HIMALAYAN QUEST

HIMALAYAN QUEST

ED VIESTURS
with PETER POTTERFIELD

NATIONAL GEOGRAPHIC
WASHINGTON, D.C.

CONTENTS

(Pages 2-3) Fantastic shapes and tendrils of moisture roil above Dhaulagiri. These beautiful clouds, known as lenticulars, are a telltale sign of extreme winds aloft—fast, high killer winds that blow over the summit of a high peak—usually the precursor of oncoming severe weather. *(Page 4)* Everest, usually a blocky peak as seen from the southerly aspect, viewed from the summit of Lhotse is a mountain of power and allure. *(Pages 6-7)* I would lose two close friends in the storm of May 10, 1996, on Everest, but we knew nothing of that as we walked through the rhododendron forest on the other side of Thyangboche. *(Pages 8-9)* The summit of Everest is frequently marked with poles left behind by various teams. The colorful prayer flags, left behind by Sherpa, contain Buddhist prayers, which are "read" by the wind and so sent aloft. *(Pages 10-11)* This shot shows the stunning view of the south side of K2 from Broad Peak. This section of our climb was so steep that we had to hack out a ledge to put up the tent. *(Pages 12-13)* This deep valley is formed by the horseshoe arrangement of the surrounding peaks—Everest, out of sight around the corner; Lhotse, just visible at the head of the valley; and Nuptse, coming in from the right—and remains completely hidden from view until you actually enter it.

CIP data located on page 160

For my wife, Paula, and my children, Gilbert and Ella,
whose love gives me strength and fills my soul

UPWARD PROGRESS

I'VE HAD THE SPECIAL PLEASURE OF STANDING ON THE SUMMIT OF MOUNT EVEREST TWICE WITH ED Viesturs: on May 23rd, 1996, and on the same date one year later. The first climb was in the aftermath of the now well-publicized tragedy that had occurred prior to our attempt to reach the summit. We documented our climb with an unwieldy IMAX® camera. In 1997, we climbed again in an attempt to understand how things could have gone so wrong the year before. This time we documented our findings with a small video camera. Both experiences revealed the remarkable ability and character of America's most accomplished and determined high-altitude climber, Ed Viesturs. Ed's ethic is rooted in craft—the

skills and judgment that he has developed through lengthy apprenticeship on lower peaks and many years of guiding around the world.

It does not surprise me that Ed Viesturs, hailing from Rockford, Illinois, has climbed more of the world's highest peaks than any other American. Ed's measured, respectful approach to climbing comes from confidence and experience, not from fear or a desire for fame. It is grounded in the unshakable conviction that mountains are not inherently dangerous places. Danger, instead, stems from inexperience, impatience, and intemperate ambition. This climbing ethic grows slowly and is hard won, for it is the knowledge that a summit holds no joy or rewards if you don't return safely. "Getting to the top is optional, but getting down is mandatory," Ed would tell me with a smile that belied his strong conviction to that principle.

Ed's quest to climb the Earth's fourteen highest summits without supplemental oxygen is not a new one—but neither is it an enterprise to be taken lightly. The peerless Tyrolean mountaineer Reinhold Messner was the first climber to achieve this remarkable feat when, in the fall of 1986, he finally reached the top of Lhotse, the final peak in his mission. The adventure took the accomplished Messner 16 years to complete.

It is probably fitting that a European should be the first to achieve this goal for it was the continental Europeans who, in the early 20th century, attached a special significance to all peaks at or above 8,000 meters (26,250 feet). Over time these peaks achieved an iconic status, not only for their great height, exotic names, and distant locations, but also because of the dramatic stories of triumph and tragedy that unfolded on their slopes. Being first on their lofty, untrodden summits was emblematic of great achievement in mountaineering, and climbing teams from around the world made daring efforts for that honor.

All of the world's 8,000-meter peaks rise in the remote border regions of Pakistan, India, Nepal, and

Tibet, arrayed in a 950-mile crescent stretching from K2 in the west to Kanchenjunga in the east. Long ago, these peaks were sediment on the floor of the Tethys Sea—until the Indian subcontinent (originally a wayward piece of the proto-continent of Gondwanaland) drifted north and collided with southern Asia. As the subcontinent slipped beneath Asia, it buckled and thrust the seafloor skyward—creating a narrow arc of mountain ranges that we call the Himalaya, a Sanskrit expression meaning "Abode of Snow."

I first met Ed some 70 million years after the seafloor first stirred, in the spring of 1987. We were traveling together to Tibet, en route to Everest's North Face. I was a member of a Swedish team, and hoped to complete the filming for a documentary on the 1920s British Mount Everest Expeditions that I'd begun the year before. Ed was a member of a Seattle-based expedition led by Eric Simonson. We

Ed Viesturs and Jim Whittaker just before Ed left Base Camp for his first Everest ascent, during 1990's International Peace Climb. Ed was honored to be under Jim's leadership for the multinational expedition to the mountain; Jim is one of his heroes.

parted ways at Base Camp and joined our respective teams. A fierce, forbidding wind scoured the mountain all of that season—neither of us reached the summit, nor did any other climber.

In 1990, we again met at the foot of Everest's North Face. Ed was a member of the International Peace Climb led by Jim Whittaker, and I was the cinematographer on a team shooting a "dramatized documentary" about the famed British climber George Mallory, who had disappeared high on the Northeast Ridge in 1924. We shared the same route but climbed on different schedules, using different camps, so I rarely saw Ed. But I did witness his grueling ascent of Everest, through the glass of the 1,000-mm lens mounted on my 16-mm motion picture camera, from the comfort of my position at Advance Base Camp (21,300 feet). The day was clear and nearly windless, and as I squinted through the eyepiece I shouted randomly to the Sherpa around me, cheering on this distant, tiny figure, lost in a sea of whiteness.

I knew that in the thin atmosphere of 28,700 feet, he would be gasping for breath, straining for every upward inch. I watched him repeat over and over the climber's high-altitude ritual: kick, kick, kick, step up, rest; kick, kick, kick, step up, rest. When he rested, I could see him hunch over his ice ax, desperately sucking at oxygen-thin air.

Three years earlier, Ed had turned back 300 feet from the summit but now, although his vertical progress was difficult to discern, I could see that he was still moving—up. As I watched the slow-motion drama unfold, I became aware that it embodied the ancient struggle between man and nature, a struggle that illuminates and exemplifies our questing, adventurous nature. High above me, a man was summoning all his strength, experience, and will in pursuit of a goal he had nurtured since his youth. Everest.

As if the ascent of Everest were not challenge enough in itself, Ed had willingly reduced his chances of success by foregoing the use of supplemental oxygen. He was adhering to his ethic of climbing the mountain "by fair means"—a principle first championed by Reinhold Messner. In our new era of anything-goes mountaineering, he wanted to play the game fairly, to test his skill and natural abilities on the mountain's terms, not his own. Entranced, I watched as his solitary figure

Rob Hall, Carlos Carsolio, and Ed Viesturs pose at Base Camp after a four-day Alpine-style ascent of Gasherbrum II.

tenaciously closed the gap between his physical limits and the summit.

It wasn't until 1996 that I had a chance to climb alongside Ed, when I invited him to join the Everest IMAX Filming Expedition as deputy leader. There's no need to recount the tragic events of that spring season—they are, by now, well known. But what is less known is the degree to which I leaned on Ed for support following the loss of our friends and acquaintances.

After the May 10 tragedy, our team returned to a windless haven in Base Camp. We gathered there for rest and solace, but we could not ignore the difficult decision we each faced: return to the mountain's wind-battered slopes, or break camp and head home. Ed reminded us that Everest doesn't have to be a death sentence, and after several days of soul-searching, careful thought, and discussion with his wife Paula, Ed decided that he would try for the summit one more time. In holding close to his ethic, he would climb without bottled oxygen even though he would be passing the bodies of fallen friends who had begun their final ascent climbing with it. It was Ed's quiet resolve and pragmatism that shored up my own morale—without it, I'm not sure I would have mustered the strength of mind to return to the mountain.

When the film team finally left the high camp on the South Col at 26,000 feet, Ed was already an hour ahead of us. He had left early to gain a head start since he was climbing "unmasked." As I struggled to find my rhythm, I often peered upward, into the unwelcoming darkness to pick out the meandering beam of Ed's headlamp. It was a bitterly cold but windless night. I monitored Ed's upward progress just as I had years before, and marveled at his extraordinary abilities.

I didn't reach Ed until I gained the South Summit at 28,710 feet, where he had waited for me. He was kneeling near Rob Hall's body. We briefly observed Rob's final resting place. No words were exchanged as we struggled to understand the events that transpired 13 days earlier. We tried to comprehend the terrible night and day that Rob had spent marooned in this lonely, wind-battered outpost. I knew that Ed had tried to prepare himself for this moment, and also for the moment when he would encounter Scott's body, lower on the mountain in the pre-dawn darkness. But I could see in his face that passing his fallen friends had taken its toll. He had shared and survived many adventures with both of them

An hour later, we both stood on the summit. Ed had arrived 20 minutes earlier. He appeared alert and focused despite the tremendous physical and mental effort he had expended. After a few photos and hugs, he was gone—headed down to the safety of the South Col, and eventually to Base Camp and Paula's outstretched arms.

The stories that follow are recounted by Ed Viesturs: a man who does not think highly of immoderate displays of pride, and a man who is not prone to exaggeration. His words and manner of storytelling are unpretentious, but do not underestimate the effort and passion that has gone into the ascents described in the pages that follow.

Finally, I would remind the reader that Ed's talents as a mountaineer are matched only by his selflessness, self-assurance, and sense of humor— qualities essential to making long and difficult expeditions memorable and rewarding. On the 1996 Everest ascent in particular, Ed's example provided inspiration and hope. We had been humbled by nature's unpredictable fury, and felt very mortal indeed. But I'll always remember Ed's presence above me as I climbed through the darkness of May 23. As he trudged indomitably upward, showing the way, dwarfed by the immensity of Everest's upper slopes.

THE THINKING MAN'S
HIGH-ALTITUDE CLIMBER

BY PETER POTTERFIELD

WHEN ED VIESTURS REACHED THE SUMMIT OF HIS FIRST 8,000-METER peak, 28,209-foot Kanchenjunga, in May 1989, he realized something. He had learned that neither the technical difficulties of the route nor the physiological challenges of high altitude had presented insurmountable problems for him—despite the fact that he had climbed without supplemental oxygen, an extreme notion at the time. It was a moment of self-discovery and one rich in potential achievement. As Viesturs lingered that day on the summit of the world's third highest peak, his gaze drifted westward

to Mount Everest, some 80 miles distant. He could see the mountain where he had been forced to turn around two years before, just 300 feet short of the world's highest summit. He felt a powerful desire to finish what he had started—and do much more, besides.

Less than a year later, Viesturs stood, alone and without the benefit of supplemental oxygen, on the summit of 29,035-foot Mount Everest. The opportunity to try Everest again had come when he was invited on the International Peace Climb for the spring of 1990. The collective goal of the climb, led by Jim Whittaker, was to put one climber from each team—the United States, China, and Russia—on the summit simultaneously. These were the years of the Cold War, and the climbers wanted to show that people from their respective countries could work together and desired peace.

Viesturs recalled reaching the summit of Everest as a dream come true. "After the years of learning and training, the months of physical and mental struggle, and near constant visualization of the moment, I could hardly believe I was actually there. I had been true to my word and true to my philosophy of climbing—to climb that mountain for what it was, and to reach its summit without the assistance of bottled oxygen."

It was also the moment that an idea began to take shape: to climb the world's highest peaks, all 14 of the mountains that stand above 8,000 meters, and to do so without supplemental oxygen. For the young American climber—30 years old at the time—the goal was entirely personal. He would try to do it his own way and without regard to external influence.

Viesturs said nothing publicly about his personal quest. He simply climbed, frequently and quietly, all over the Himalaya, gaining strength, experience, and judgment with each ascent. That was especially true of K2. A few hundred meters lower than Mount Everest, the "savage mountain" of Pakistan's Karakoram Range is universally considered to be more difficult, and far more dangerous. Viesturs traveled there in 1992 with American

climber Scott Fischer, and immediately their attempt devolved into a series of deadly trials and frustrations. But with characteristic tenacity, after two months of struggle on the second highest peak in the world, Viesturs and Fischer stood on top of K2— and survived a harrowing descent. Besides proving the importance of persistence, the long expedition had done something else: It brought Viesturs together with New Zealand climber Rob Hall, who would become a close friend and partner.

The seasons to come would be some of the most successful ever for any Himalayan climber. In a span of only 20 months, Ed Viesturs climbed six of the world's highest peaks. In 1994, he reached the summit of Everest for the third time and less than a week later reached the summit of Lhotse, the fourth highest peak in the world. That was in the spring; in the autumn of that year he climbed Cho Oyu, the sixth

In 1997, David Breashears shot the film Into the Death Zone *for NOVA, a documentary detailing high-altitude physiology while climbing Mount Everest. The climbing team is shown just leaving the summit, a part of the route that calls for great care. Clearly visible in this photograph is the corniced ridge to the left. Climbers need to keep well inside of the cornices and stay mentally focused on each step. With the Southwest Face on the right and the Kangshung Face on the left, any slip will likely be a fatal one.*

highest peak in the world. Six months later, in the spring of 1995, Viesturs was turned back by dangerous snow conditions and high winds near the summit of Everest, but he traveled immediately to Makalu, just east of Everest, where he climbed "big Mac," the fifth highest mountain in the world. A month later Viesturs journeyed to the Karakoram with Rob Hall and climbed two more of the world's highest peaks, Gasherbrum I (Hidden Peak) and Gasherbrum II.

His was a stunning record of ascents. The fact he had suffered no serious mishaps during those years of maximum effort in what may be the most dangerous landscapes on the planet reinforced Viesturs's confidence in his own unique abilities. He kept climbing. By the autumn of 2002, he had accomplished most of what he set out to do more than a decade earlier: He had climbed to the summit of 12 of the world's 14 highest peaks and to the top of Everest five times. For the even-tempered Viesturs, the rewards for this achievement still come entirely from within.

"The only reason I climb is for my own personal satisfaction," he has said. "I love the challenge. I feel incredibly lucky to be doing what I love. That's rare in life. Going to the summit is what it's all about, but if I have to turn around for safety reasons, that's fine with me. We can always try again. The important thing is to go, to have that experience, to be in that landscape, to spend time on those mountains—and to give it everything you've got.

"The fact I'm still not done yet," he added, "shows how hard this is. It's clearly a challenge worthy of my best efforts. And the fact I'm still climbing more than a decade later proves how much fun it is."

Part of what draws Viesturs to high-altitude climbing is his unusual physiology. Clinical laboratory studies show he processes oxygen better, more quickly, and in bigger volumes than most of us. It became apparent during his very first climbs in the Himalaya. Above 26,000 or even 27,000 feet, he seemed less debilitated than most of the other guys around him. That extraordinary capability and a high level of aerobic fitness combine with the less tangible realities of long experience and refined judgment. The result is a climber who can both perform physically and think clearly in the rarefied air of the highest mountains on the planet.

Viesturs's experience on Himalayan peaks gives him a perspective that translates into an ability to relate to others what it's like to be there. His gift at articulating his experiences in that hypoxic landscape of deadly cold and dangerous terrain has set him apart from other climbers and created an audience that is fascinated with high-altitude climbing. What the public gets from Viesturs are thoughtful and articulate remarks about the realities of his workplace: joy, fear, avalanches, steep ice, heart-stopping sunrises, whiteouts at 28,000 feet, hurricane-force winds, and wrenching decisions to retreat.

"The capability in recent years to share what I do with others has brought more people into the world of high-altitude climbing," notes Viesturs. "Through films, photographs, lectures and slide shows, and my live dispatches via the Internet, I'm able to transfer some of the excitement I feel to people who are deeply interested. In a way, that sharing in words and images makes what I do less selfish, and more rewarding."

In the insular world of mountaineering, Viesturs's standing as an accomplished—and intelligent—climber derives from his success on the highest mountains on Earth. But he became America's best known high-altitude climber through exposure in other media—lectures, Internet dispatches from the Himalaya, the feature film *Vertical Limit,* and documentary projects such as the IMAX film *Everest* and the NOVA film *Into the Death Zone.* During both the latter film projects, in 1996 and 1997 respectively, Viesturs climbed Everest on cue. "The IMAX expedition itself was difficult," said Viesturs. "Climbing Everest is never easy, but that year our days were twice as long as normal. You couldn't just climb, you had to stop, wait for the right light, wait for the camera to be set up, start the scene—then the camera would run out of film. So you'd have to stop, reload the camera, and start all over. It was frustrating in some respects, but we all realized that this is what we were there for: not just to climb the mountain, but to make the film so that others can see what it's like."

The grueling work of making the film was to be disrupted and almost derailed by the tragic events of May 10, 1996, when a sudden storm blew in high on the mountain and took the lives of eight climbers. That day, film expedition members at Camp II could see parties still on the summit ridge late. Viesturs began to worry that the climbers would run out of oxygen. He then watched with rising concern as the weather began to change.

Then the big afternoon storm moved in. The IMAX team heard nothing from the climbers at or above Camp IV. Finally, Ed Viesturs's wife, Paula, radioed the IMAX expedition at Camp II later that evening from Base Camp with ghastly news: Only half the people had returned to Camp IV. That meant as many as 12 to 14 people were missing somewhere below the summit.

The next days revealed the full extent of the tragedy: Rob Hall and Scott Fischer, both close friends to Viesturs, perished in the storm, along with six other climbers. After participating in the rescue of some of the survivors, Breashears and Viesturs and the other team members considered carefully whether to continue making the film or to go home.

"I was devastated at the loss of my friends," Viesturs said, "but I didn't want to leave. I felt that if we left the mountain in the wake of that tragedy, we would leave this pall of death over the mountain; people would think Everest is this killer mountain. But mountains don't kill people, they just sit there, and it's your own actions that result in either a good or deadly experience. I wanted to show people that we could safely climb the mountain and safely come back down. The other team members agreed with that."

On May 22, their commitment paid off. By then, after 50 days on the mountain, the team members were well acclimated. All that remained was to shoot footage above Camp III. On summit day, Viesturs was the only one on the team to climb without oxygen, so he left an hour earlier. The plan was for the film crew to catch Ed somewhere above the Balcony at 27,600 feet. Viesturs left Camp IV at 11 p.m., climbing alone into a "beautiful" night. But he climbed so fast the rest of the crew never caught up with him; the record of his summit that day is not a couple of hundred feet of 70-mm film stock but a portrait taken on top with a camera.

"I felt so great, I felt really strong," Viesturs recalled. "I was pumped to go to the summit. It was the strongest day I ever spent in the mountains, but also one of the saddest."

The climb held a macabre element. On his way up, Viesturs passed the body of Scott Fischer and later came upon that of Rob Hall. Viesturs recalls seeing the bodies of his friends with sadness: "There were emotions I had never felt before. I had never had a friend die, let alone a climbing partner. So seeing my friends' bodies was very difficult. Coming down, all I could do was sit there, spend some time with them. For days before that, I had cried and talked about this tragedy with others, so that was psychologically helpful by the time I saw them. But it was a strange and sad feeling. To this day I still don't know how to adequately describe it."

Viesturs, who had a long apprenticeship as a guide on Mount Rainier while studying to become a veterinarian, is no stranger to the dangers of climbing and the tragedy that can ensue. But he has studied how best to gauge the risk of objective dangers—avalanches, falling rocks, the sorts of realities where all the skill in the world can't help you. A combination of skill and judgment is his most valuable asset on a big mountain. Carefully applied, he says, it can reduce risk. He makes decisions accordingly—and understands the consequences of those decisions.

Viesturs failed on only one expedition—on K2—to maintain a rigorous commitment to good judgment and has resolved never to take what he considers "such unreasonable" risks again. He's a proponent of smart climbing who urges other climbers to exercise careful judgment; he's not reluctant to set an example by turning back.

In 1998, Viesturs and Finnish climber Veikka Gustafsson were close to the summit of 26,795-foot Dhaulagiri when they encountered obvious avalanche conditions. They spent two or three nights at high camp waiting for conditions to change. Finally they got a calm, clear night, a beautiful night for climbing. But slab avalanche potential 1,500 feet below the top turned them back. They looked at each other and knew the smart call was to go down.

It is hard to turn your back and climb down after investing weeks or months of effort and a lot of money. That's especially true when the summit is mere hours away, making for a deadly temptation.

"No summit is worth dying for," said Viesturs. "If I encounter conditions on a climb that indicate a high probability of avalanche or other danger I can't control, I'm going to turn around no matter how close I am. You can always come back to try again—unless you decide to press on and get killed. It's that simple. Reaching the summit is optional; getting down is mandatory."

Willingness to "bail today and try again another day" has proved effective. In 1993, Viesturs made an attempt on Shishapangma (Xixabangma), climbing alone to the Central Summit of the sprawling, elegant peak, less than 20 vertical feet below the 26,286-foot true summit. But he judged the snow conditions along the 100-yard traverse to the Main Summit to be unsafe. He turned and went down. Eight years later, in 2001, he returned with Gustafsson. That season the pair found excellent conditions and together climbed to the true summit of the world's 14th highest peak.

After their retreat on Dhaulagiri in 1998, Viesturs and Gustafsson returned to the peak the next season. But this time the climbers hoped for more than just another attempt on Dhaulagiri: They planned to climb two 8,000-meter peaks within days of each other.

Climbing two or even three 8,000-meter peaks back to back can make a lot of sense if you're physically able to handle it. The advantage comes with acclimatization. Once your body has adjusted to the low-oxygen atmosphere at high altitude, you're better able to function. So, going from one high peak to another is not so outlandish as it might sound. And since you're already acclimatized, with acceptable weather it's sometimes possible to climb the second peak in Alpine style—in a single push.

Viesturs set out in spring 1999 to climb two relatively remote Himalayan giants. With Gustafsson, he hoped to climb Manaslu and then move quickly to Dhaulagiri and try again on that peak.

Manaslu, a seldom-climbed mountain tucked away in a corner of the Himalaya, was something of a mystery to Viesturs and Gustafsson. The route had been done but it wasn't well documented; there wasn't a line on the map that said, "go here." The pair, without the help of Sherpa climbers, forged a route across mixed ground, straightforward glaciers, and dangerous icefalls. Placing three camps along the route, they reached the top on the 12th day of their climb, despite a cold and windy summit day. "The snow was so hard, our crampons barely dented the surface," remembered Viesturs, "but as far as speed was concerned, you could fly. Our motivation was up the whole time, and we climbed in perfect unison to the top. It was a memorable day for us." The two men stood alone on the summit of the eighth highest mountain on Earth. Instead of climbing down, packing up, and going home, the pair returned to a village below their Base Camp. From there, they flew by helicopter to Dhaulagiri. The travel technique saved weeks of trekking and preserved the acclimatization earned on Manaslu.

Viesturs, by then a connoisseur of Himalayan peaks, was delighted to find they had Dhaulagiri (the seventh highest mountain in the world) entirely to themselves. The solitude was a far cry from the crowds so often encountered on Everest. The climbers put everything they'd need for the ascent into their packs and with 42-pound loads set off from Base Camp. They spent the first night at 20,000 feet and carried their tent as high as they could get the following day—24,000 feet. Early that next morning, the climbers set out on a steep traverse leading to the broad summit ridge. By 11 a.m. the pair was on top, having climbed an 8,000-meter peak in three days, like weekend climbers doing a route in the Rockies.

But success like that doesn't come with every Himalayan season. If there's one quality that sets Viesturs apart from other climbers, it is his confidence in his ability to judge conditions, decide on an appropriate course of action, and then live with those decisions. "As you get older," Viesturs explained, "you get smarter. Making the tough decisions becomes easier because you're able to see the consequences more clearly and to better withstand external pressure. An 8,000-meter peak is no place to let others decide whether to go up or down, because it's your life that's at stake."

Viesturs, who by 2000 had already climbed eleven 8,000-meter peaks, described his first journey to Annapurna as "coming home." Climbing with Veikka Gustafsson, Michael Kennedy, and Neil Beidleman, Viesturs was dismayed to find that conditions on the storied peak made the climb of their proposed north-side route untenable. "The objective danger was just off the scale," Viesturs recalled. "The upper part of the mountain was completely blocked by ice cliffs. To travel underneath that stuff day in and day out was insane. Some people might accept conditions like that, but I won't. We spent a lot of time and looked at many different routes, but nothing was acceptable to any of us. We came home."

Viesturs returned to Annapurna in the spring of 2002, but this time to a different side. He hoped that a long, high route on the south side of the peak, even though it put the climbers at greater risk of weather and altitude for much of the route, would prove more feasible than the avalanche-prone line they had attempted two years earlier.

From the south side they hoped to get on the East Ridge of Annapurna. From there to the summit is a long ridge, between 7,000 and 8,000 meters along its length. The route goes up and over the East Summit and Central Summit of Annapurna before reaching the Main Summit. It makes for a long time in the Death Zone. It was a compromise: There was less objective danger, but they would have to spend more time up high. For Ed, the option offered more control.

But after weeks of climbing on the route, Viesturs encountered conditions that to his experienced eye revealed a deadly danger. "A feature called Roc Noir, about 24,000 feet, has an 800-foot snow face of about 45 degrees," Viesturs explained. "It is very prone to avalanche. That day, it was a textbook avalanche slope. The level of risk was unacceptable. It's a tough call to make when you spend four or five weeks on an expedition like that, and you get so close. But I've done it before, and I may have to do it again. When it feels bad, and my gut instinct is telling me it is bad, then I know it's bad."

"You can't eliminate the risk of climbing Himalayan peaks," Viesturs added. "Mountains are potentially dangerous. But you can avoid walking right into the most blatant and obvious risks. The key is understanding the consequences of each decision—and keeping a sense of perspective. For me, it's all about the journey, not the summit itself."

THE MEMORY OF PHOTOGRAPHS

YEARS AGO, I BECAME INSPIRED TO CLIMB MOUNTAINS AFTER READING THE BOOK *Annapurna*. The mountaineering classic is Maurice Herzog's eloquent account of the 1950 French expedition that became the first to reach the summit of an 8,000-meter peak. I was inspired not only by the words describing the epic ascent but also by the accompanying photos, which effectively transported me to the frozen slopes of the Himalayan giant. Other stories and photos have since moved me in much the same way. The sheer awe-inspiring beauty and raw power of high mountains—which can best be seen through the eyes of a climber at extreme altitudes—still

motivate and intrigue me. Now a seasoned veteran of Himalayan expeditions, I have seen such beautiful mountain landscapes through my own eyes. The memories of those many attempts on mountain summits, and the treasured moments spent with friends along the way, are indelible.

There can be no real substitute for those mental images; they are memory itself. But photographs help refresh the memories of special times, beautiful places, and unforgettable people. Fortunately, through the years I have had the foresight to capture my mountaineering adventures on film. I went to this trouble—at altitude, photography is a tremendous and tedious effort—for my own benefit, and to share those events with family and friends. As a professional climber, I find these images serve yet another purpose: They help me tell the tale of my adventures to those who have an interest in the strange world of high-altitude climbing. The photographs themselves may best explain to others what it is I do.

Himalayan Quest is the result of 15 years of photography in the Himalaya. By sharing these images, I can give others an opportunity to see the beautiful things I have seen, often from the highest points on Earth. I selected these particular photographs not necessarily for their artistic merits, but for their significance to me and their ability to convey a sense of place. The editing process was not an easy one. In file cabinets full of plastic sheets of stored slides, there were so many images from which to choose I could have filled a dozen books. In the end, I returned to the images that I have always regarded as my favorites. I chose photographs that most accurately mirrored the memory of the moment—the moment that I saw, was moved by, and tried to capture on film.

These images will share with others what I have been lucky to see. Through a decade and a half of climbing in the Himalaya, I have traveled to amazing places where few human beings ever go and have seen sights seldom viewed by others. These views remain a part of what draws me to the mountains: the indescribable

beauty of a sunrise from 28,000 feet; ethereal mists parting to reveal a Himalayan peak; the alpenglow of sunset from high camp; and the world far below as seen from the summits of the highest peaks on Earth.

I would not consider myself in the league of great outdoor photographers such as Art Wolfe or the late Galen Rowell. These people are true artists, completely committed to the act of creating an image. My photography, by comparison, is incidental. What I do is climb mountains, and that's where my focus must lie. But I choose to carry a camera as well and to document what I can while still being focused on the climbing. My photographic equipment is good, but simple: one camera and one lens, and neither of those too heavy or too complicated. There is no way I could consider carrying an array of camera bodies, lenses, and filters to the mountain summits I strive to reach.

After a months-long expedition climbing the 8,000-meter peaks in the Karakoram of Pakistan, climbers feel a certain sensory deprivation. But there's a place on the long trek out, just above Askole, where the returning climber is just knocked out by the sudden vision of a beautiful sea of green, a lush landscape of hand-irrigated fields. Along with the view comes the wonderful aroma of earth and vegetation. The temperature is warm, the air is soft; returning here is like coming back to life.

Though perhaps not obvious to those who do not climb, photography at altitude is difficult. At lower elevations one typically has the luxury of a saturated atmosphere, mental acuity, more or less level ground, and warm fingers. One can focus on the minutiae of photography. But at extreme altitude, one's focus must lie elsewhere—on survival. Hundreds of potentially beautiful images are never recorded because it is simply too difficult or even dangerous. The slope may be too steep and precarious, the air too thin and cold, or the situation too desperate. There were times when the task at hand—plodding and gasping my way up through deep snow at 26,000 feet—was all that I could bear.

The reality of climbing at altitude has left me with memories of countless places I wished I had captured on film, but the urge to take photographs was pushed aside as a distraction or a waste of precious energy, a thought that could not be so much as entertained. The instant would pass, along with the opportunity. For me, when the choice is either to climb or to take pictures, climbing wins out. There were times, however, when I saw something so powerful that I could not resist. I forced myself to stop, break my train of thought, halt my steady and deliberate pace, and try to grab the shot. I am thankful for those moments and the images that resulted.

I am also grateful for the physiological gift of being able to function relatively well at extreme altitude. Having adequate strength sufficient not only to climb without supplemental oxygen but also to maintain an acute awareness of my surroundings and my own physical condition has allowed me to safely ascend and descend the biggest mountains on Earth. This strength has also helped me maintain sufficient control and awareness in that wild environment to be able to take photographs.

Some of the images in this collection are simple landscapes that moved me. Some are portraits of interesting people that I met along the way. Others were taken up high while climbing. Some were shot on the actual summits of 8,000-meter peaks. Together, they show the world of the high-altitude climber. A few of these images are slightly out of focus because of a frost-covered lens or an unsteady hand. Some show horizons that are not exactly level, or exposure a little off perfect. I believe these effects, which may be seen as shortcomings, are instead revealing of the moment and lend authenticity to the events that were captured.

The dawn photo of Scott Fischer high on K2 is such an example. It was extremely cold; the sun had just risen. I was hanging with one hand to my ice ax at the top of the steep and icy Bottleneck Couloir, 27,000 feet up on what is probably the most dangerous mountain in the Himalaya. I feel lucky to have taken the photo at all, and I am not bothered by the soft focus captured by the frosty lens. To me, this lends a chilling aura, a sense of reality, to the shot. The result speaks for itself. I will forever remember the ascent of K2 with Scott Fischer and the force of will that gave us the strength to climb this mighty Himalayan peak.

One of my favorite images shows a shadow cast by Everest. I took that photo at 28,000 feet on the Southeast Ridge during my ascent in 1997. This was the fifth time in my career that I had passed this way, but never had I seen such an awe-inspiring scene. In fact, I never had been so high on Everest so early in the morning. It was approximately 4:30 a.m., and we were well on our way to the summit. Our team had left Camp IV at the South Col six and a half hours earlier to escape the crowds of other climbers who also hoped to climb to the summit that day. The events of May 10, 1996, still haunted David Breashears, Pete Athans, and me, and we felt that with so many people once again vying for the top, we needed to be well ahead to avoid potential problems. The early start for the summit push put me in a rare position—so high, so early. It was bone-chillingly cold, and the effort it took to stop and compose a photograph was significant. But this was a moment I wanted very much to preserve.

A picture of my wife, Paula, and Araceli Segarra, David Breashears, and myself immediately after the 1996 Everest IMAX Filming Expedition reflects a very poignant moment. I set my camera on timer to take the image. We had just arrived in the village of

Deboche after a long day trekking from Everest Base Camp. We had been on the mountain for ten of the most demanding weeks of my life. Not only had we been consumed with our task of climbing the peak and filming the ascent with the monstrous IMAX camera, we also had been thrown into the most tragic mountaineering disaster of recent times. We had lost friends and had helped rescue others. Despite what happened, we made our ascent and we made the film. During this long process we consumed more emotional and physical energy than perhaps we possessed. Looking back, I cannot imagine where our drive came from to finish that project.

Arriving in Deboche, we realized finally that we were done—our task completed. For the first time in many months we could relax, and this photo shows the relief and happiness of the moment. We hid the sadness and disbelief of what we had just experienced. The loss of Rob Hall and Scott Fischer left a huge gap and deeply affected all of us. These were great men and dear friends.

Some of the photos in this collection are self-portraits. I have on several occasions found myself alone high on a peak or on the actual summit. A summit self-portrait offers no opportunity for great photography: All you can do is mount the camera on an ice ax or ski pole, set the timer, and try to get in the frame. For me, the self-portrait is more of a celebration of the achievement than a proof to others that I was on the summit. Nonetheless, one must acknowledge that that "proof" is extremely important to some.

My first summit of Everest was recorded with a self-portrait. I was alone on the top—in a moment that I had dreamed of for so long. As I took it all in, the reality of where I was, I could scarcely believe that my dream of climbing Everest without oxygen had come true. It was such a personal moment that I was happy to be alone, glad to have that selfish moment to myself. I had a special camera clamp that attached to the top of my ice ax, which I could drive straight into the snow to provide a stable monopod for my camera. Quickly working without gloves, I set the auto-timer, prayed that the camera would set the correct exposure, guessed at the focus distance, pressed the shutter button, stumbled back to the summit somewhere in front of the camera, and hoped for the best.

The results took my breath away. My first summit of Everest was frozen in time on film. By no means a perfect photo, the shot was thankfully in focus, if slightly overexposed, and I somehow had placed myself directly in front of the camera. All of this at 29,028 feet in a space the size of a large dining-room table. (In 1990 the summit of Everest was thought to be 29,028 feet, an elevation that was revised in 1999 to 29,035 feet. I am glad I climbed Everest when it was lower!) I have had that picture on my office wall ever since it came back from processing.

After my expeditions, I confess to waiting with unease and even trepidation while my film is being developed. The moment of truth draws near: Did the camera malfunction? Did I forget to load the film? Was my bulky mittened thumb in front of the lens? On some few occasions, those very misfortunes have occurred. As a result, I have felt hugely disappointed. But I take solace in the fact that I am a climber, not a photographer. I cannot go back in time—nor would I want to go all the way back up to the place where the lost shots should have been taken. I realize that they are images that will reside only in my memory and leave it at that. They are the photographs I cannot share.

Some of the shots that I did manage to squeeze out of my frozen camera are displayed in this book. I hope they will transport you to the high Himalaya and perhaps inspire and intrigue you as well.

ED VIESTURS
September 2002

HIMALAYAN QUEST
ED VIESTURS

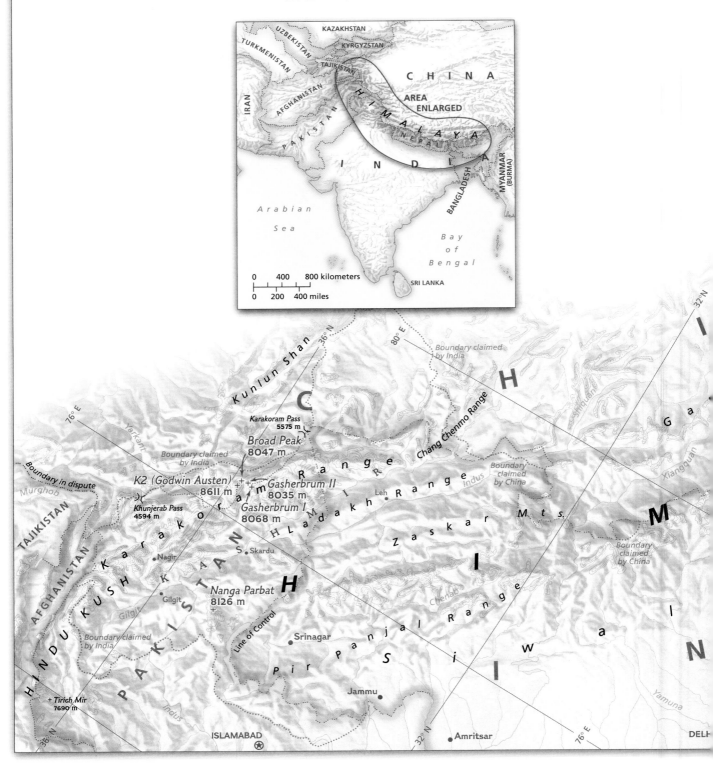

KAZAKHSTAN

UZBEKISTAN

TURKMENISTAN

KYRGYZSTAN

TAJIKISTAN

C H I N A

IRAN

AFGHANISTAN

AREA
ENLARGED

PAKISTAN

H I M A L A Y A

NEPAL

I N D I A

MYANMAR
(BURMA)

BANGLADESH

Arabian
Sea

Bay
of
Bengal

SRI LANKA

0   400   800 kilometers

0   200   400 miles

Boundary claimed
by India

32° N

Kunlun Shan

36° N

80° E

H

C

Ga

76° E

Yarkant

Karakoram Pass
5575 m

Broad Peak
8047 m

Range

Chang Chenmo Range

Boundary
claimed
by China

Xiangquan

Boundary claimed
by India

K2 (Godwin Austen)
8611 m

Gasherbrum II
8035 m

Leh

Ladakh Range

M

Murghob

Boundary in dispute

Khunjerab Pass
4594 m

Karako

Gasherbrum I
8068 m

H L a

Indus

Mts.

Boundary
claimed
by China

TAJIKISTAN

S. Skardu

Z a s k a r

AFGHANISTAN

HINDU

Nagir

P A K I S T A N

I

KUSH

Karako

Gilgit

Nanga Parbat
8126 m

H

Chenab

Gilgit

Srinagar

Pir Panjal Range

W

N

Line of Control

S

i

Boundary claimed
by India

Tirich Mir
7690 m

Indus

Jammu

Yamuna

36° N

ISLAMABAD

32° N

Amritsar

76° E

DELHI

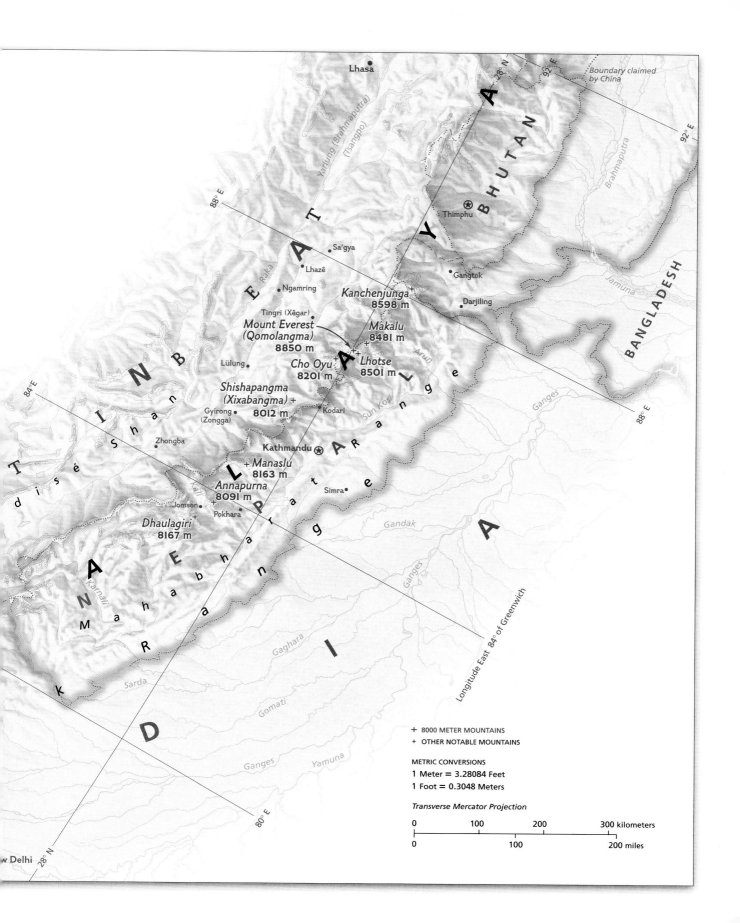

Lhasa

Boundary claimed
by China

92° E

Yarlung (Brahmaputra)
(Tsangpo)

88° E

G R E A T

B H U T A N

Thimphu

Y

Sa'gya
Lhazê

Ngamring

Kanchenjunga
8598 m

Gangtok

Darjiling

Tingri (Xêgar)

Mount Everest
(Qomolangma)
8850 m

Makalu
8481 m

Lülung

Cho Oyu
8201 m

H A

Lhotse
8501 m

Arun

Shishapangma
(Xixabangma)
8012 m

Kodari

L

Gyirong
(Zongga)

Sun Kosi

Zhongba

Kathmandu

A R

a

n

g

Ganges

88° E

BANGLADESH

Jamuna

Brahmaputra

Raka

T I B

N

I S

H A

T

I S

Disê

d

Manaslu
8163 m

P r a t

Annapurna
8091 m

Jomson

Pokhara

Simra

e

Gandak

Ganges

Dhaulagiri
8167 m

Kali

A

g

84° E

M A

E

N

M a h a b h a r a t

Karnali

R

Gaghara

I

A

Longitude East 84° of Greenwich

K

Sarda

D

Gomati

Ganges

Yamuna

80° E

w Delhi   28° N

+ 8000 METER MOUNTAINS
+ OTHER NOTABLE MOUNTAINS

METRIC CONVERSIONS
1 Meter = 3.28084 Feet
1 Foot = 0.3048 Meters

Transverse Mercator Projection

| 0 | 100 | 200 | 300 kilometers |

| 0 | 100 | 200 miles |

28° N

CHAPTER ONE

EVEREST GREAT COULOIR
EVEREST EAST FACE

THE YEAR 1987 WAS A MAJOR MILESTONE FOR ME. IT WAS THE YEAR OF my first expedition to the Himalaya—to Mount Everest. I was invited by Eric Simonson, who had been to the north side of the mountain before. For me, it was all new: the flight to Kathmandu, the long journey through Tibet to the Rongbuk Glacier, those first amazing views of Everest.

We made our attempt via the North Face. Our summit push took us into the Great Couloir. Eric and I got to a point above 28,500 feet. We were on track for the summit but had fixed all of our rope to get to that point. We began climbing unroped and traversed toward the upper part of the West Ridge where the climbing became quite technical. We could manage the difficulties on the upper part of the West Ridge all the way to the summit, but we knew we couldn't descend safely without a rope. So, 300 feet below the summit we turned around and came down.

I made my second journey to Mount Everest in 1988 with Andy Politz, who had guided with me for years on Mount Rainier. Our objective was to climb the East Face, which may be the most difficult and dangerous on the mountain. After a few weeks I realized that the attempt was not in line with my philosophy of climbing. Seracs and ice cliffs on Lhotse continually showered the route with debris. The face was blatantly dangerous, and so no fun at all to climb. We turned to an Alpine-style ascent of Kartse instead.

KARTSE *21,000 feet | 6,405 meters* Andy Politz descends Kartse after the two of us made a fast ascent of the 21,500-foot peak. We turned to Kartse after the route we had hoped to climb on Everest—the daunting East Face—proved unsafe. This photograph symbolizes the kind of photography I aspire to do: documenting remote corners of the Himalaya. In the distance, this image shows a side of a major peak—in this case, the striking North Face of Makalu—which most people have never seen.

EAST FACE OF EVEREST
(PRECEDING PAGES) In 1988, I made my second journey to Mount Everest, this time with Andy Politz, who had guided with me for years on Mount Rainier. Our objective was to climb the East Face. After a few weeks on the route, I realized that the attempt was not in line with my philosophy of climbing. The face was too dangerous. So instead, we turned to a consolation prize: Andy and I made an Alpine-style ascent of Kartse. The climb was spectacular; while we were on the summit, we watched the sun rise to bathe Everest in morning pastels. The East Face of Everest in such flattering dawn light was one of the most spectacular sights I have seen in the Himalaya.

CHOMO-LONZO,
FROM TIBET

(OPPOSITE) I took this photograph of Andy Politz gazing at Chomo-lonzo on our way to the East Face of Everest in 1988. This is a special shot in that it conveys the essence of being "out there." We were in the remote Kharta Valley on the Tibetan (eastern) side of Everest. This valley was first explored by George Mallory and his teammates in the 1920s as they searched for a feasible route to the summit of Everest. Even today, this part of the range is rarely visited and exudes an aura of wilderness.

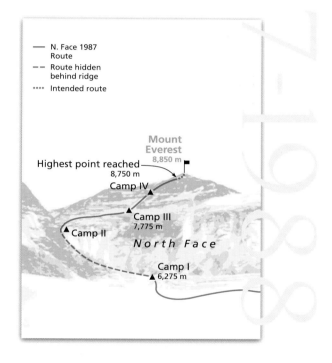

—— N. Face 1987 Route
– – Route hidden behind ridge
···· Intended route

Mount Everest 8,850 m
Highest point reached 8,750 m
Camp IV
Camp III 7,775 m
Camp II
North Face
Camp I 6,275 m

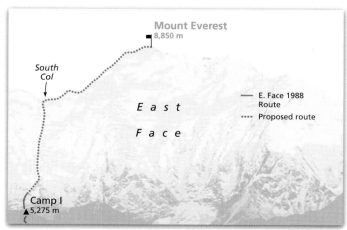

Mount Everest 8,850 m
South Col
East Face
—— E. Face 1988 Route
···· Proposed route
Camp I 5,275 m

CHAPTER TWO

KANCHENJUNGA

A YEAR AFTER MY ATTEMPT ON THE EAST FACE OF MOUNT EVEREST, I was invited on an expedition led by Lou Whittaker to Kanchenjunga. This was to be a congenial expedition, but one that was focused and successful, too. The team was made up primarily of guides from Mount Rainier—George Dunn, Phil Ershler, Greg Wilson—and included two other climbers I admire, John Roskelley and Jim Wickwire. It was a great experience, partly because we attempted a hard, steep route on the third highest mountain in the world and still managed to put six people on the summit. This was the first full-blown American expedition to Kanchenjunga, though Carlos Buhler had become the first American to climb the peak several years before.

The route we chose to climb ascends the steep Northwest Face, with substantial sections of technical climbing leading to the North Ridge at 24,000 feet. Even with such a strong expedition, it took two weeks to lead and fix ropes for this portion of the climb. Many of the key sections were led by John Roskelley and Larry Nielson. We fixed between 3,000 and 4,000 feet of rope on this face, which was composed of mixed rock and ice at 40° to 50°. At 1 p.m. on May 21, 1989, I stood on the summit of Kanchenjunga, my first 8,000-meter peak.

NORTHWEST FACE, KANCHENJUNGA   *21,000 feet | 6,405 meters* Steep ice characterizes the Northwest Face of Kanchenjunga. This shot by George Dunn shows Phil Ershler ascending the fixed ropes on the Northwest Face. The base of this section started at 21,000 feet and crested at the North Ridge at 24,000 feet. We fixed a few thousand feet of rope on this face for obvious reasons: It is steep and technical.

KANCHENJUNGA SUMMIT

28,209 feet | 8,598 meters

(PRECEDING PAGES) I stood on the summit of Kanchenjunga and took this photo of my companions coming up behind me. Craig Van Hoy can be seen belaying Phil Ershler to the top of the third highest peak on the planet. We're climbing out of a sea of afternoon clouds, clearly visible far below. The highest point of the summit is to the left and just out of the photo. We chose not to take the final few steps to the actual summit, which is considered sacred to the people of the surrounding valleys. We could have walked up to it in a minute, but the locals asked us not to disturb that area and we respected their wishes. We spent a wonderful hour in calm and sunny conditions on the summit, enjoying our success and taking in the view.

NEPALESE BOY

(OPPOSITE) A young boy stares in wonder as our plane, departing the Kanchenjunga area, leaves the small, grassy airstrip in his village Taplejung. This youth made a deep impression on me. His home was in that remote village, where he led a simple, and, in some respects very good, existence. I have traveled enough in Nepal to know how close and warm family ties are there. But I also knew this child's opportunities were limited, which is why his fascination with the airplanes—he seemed transfixed by them—struck me. He stood there and watched intently as the Twin Otters flew in and out with our expedition gear. It's quite probable he will never fly in a plane, ride in a car, or visit the distant city of Kathmandu.

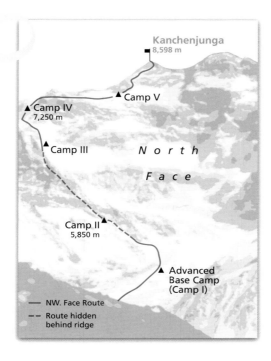

Kanchenjunga
■ 8,598 m

▲ Camp V

▲ Camp IV
7,250 m

▲ Camp III

North Face

▲ Camp II
5,850 m

▲ Advanced Base Camp (Camp I)

— NW. Face Route

-- Route hidden behind ridge

KANCHENJUNGA SUMMIT
28,209 feet | 8,598 meters

(LEFT) The summit of Kanchenjunga is one of the great vantage points in the entire range. We were fortunate enough to be there on a cloudless, glorious day in the high Himalaya. The three main peaks on the far horizon are Makalu, Lhotse, and Everest. Just to the right of Everest is Cho Oyu. Two years earlier I had been on Everest with Eric Simonson, but we were turned back just 300 feet from the summit while climbing up the Great Couloir. And here I was on the summit of Kanchenjunga, looking at Everest, remembering my failure there, and knowing I desperately wanted to go back and finish that last 300 feet. I got the opportunity: When we got down from this climb, Lou Whittaker, our expedition leader, called his brother Jim, who told Lou that I had been accepted to go to Everest with him the next year for the International Peace Climb.

KANCHENJUNGA
27,500 feet | 8,387 meters

(FOLLOWING PAGES) Sunrise is frequently the best part of any climbing day for me, especially if I am on my way toward the summit. We had already been climbing for a few hours, and as we gained elevation—here we're at about 27,500 feet—the sun rose and afforded this impressive view toward the west. Alpenglow bathes the surrounding peaks in oranges and reds. It's amazing how that burst of ethereal color gives me a psychological strength that is sorely lacking in the cold and dark of our alpine starts. The crunch of the snow underfoot and the rasp of our labored breathing were the only sounds of the calm morning, the beginning of a spectacular summit day. The closer sunlit peak on the left is the West Peak of Kanchenjunga—a difficult climb in its own right. The two smaller peaks in the distant left horizon are Lhotse and Everest, about 80 miles away. The fluted face of Pyramid Peak can be seen at lower right. The view is to the north and west, toward Tibet.

CHAPTER THREE

EVEREST NORTH RIDGE

WHEN I GOT DOWN FROM THE SUMMIT OF KANCHENJUNGA, Lou Whittaker told me his brother Jim had invited me on the International Peace Climb for 1990, an expedition to be made up of Russian, American, and Chinese climbers. The idea was to promote peace through climbing, and Jim, who had been the first American to summit Everest, did a great job holding everything together. With a diverse crew with different climbing styles and methodologies, that wasn't easy.

Jim's rule was that the first team use supplemental oxygen so that their team had a high chance of success, and so that all 6 members would arrive roughly at the same time. He wanted me on the first team, but since I refused to use oxygen we agreed that I would go on the second. I was alone because my two Soviet partners had been climbing with oxygen and so moved faster. They had already gone to the summit and started down. It was a great achievement for me to get there by myself.

Taking the last steps to the summit was fantastic. The implication was clear: If I could climb Everest without oxygen, I could perhaps climb them all. The day before, two Americans, two Russians, and two Chinese reached the top—that was the whole idea, to get climbers from each country to the summit simultaneously. The weather stayed good and Jim kept sending people up. The atmosphere was "Go! Go! Go!" We got 20 people to the summit, in spurts of varying numbers.

FIRST SUMMIT *29,035 feet | 8,850 meters* **On May 8, 1990, at 1 p.m., I finally stood on the summit of Everest—a dream come true. After the years of learning and training, months of physical and mental struggle, and near constant visualization of the moment, I could hardly believe I was actually there. I had climbed to the highest point on Earth without the use of supplemental oxygen. Being alone on top was fine with me, because this was a very personal moment, one that would have been difficult to share.**

| XEGAR, TIBET

On my first trip to Everest in 1987, Eric Simonson and I went to climb the Great Couloir. For climbs on the north side of Mount Everest, you usually start from Kathmandu, then drive up to Kodari on the border between Nepal and Chinese Tibet. From there, you drive dusty roads toward the northern approaches to Everest. Xegar is one of the places you pass along the way. There are the remnants of a Buddhist monastery that was destroyed by the Chinese. We climbed a little hill nearby and found this small cairn with a tower where pilgrims come. The thing was loaded with prayer flags, and to see them whipping around in the wind in the middle of that barren landscape was eerie.

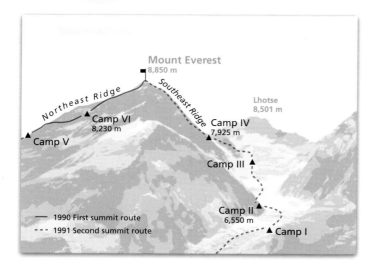

1992

I N 1992, I WENT TO K2 TO CLIMB WITH SCOTT FISCHER ON A JOURNEY THAT SAW big problems from the start. We had trouble raising money and our original expedition plans collapsed. In the end, we signed on with a Russian expedition that had some openings on their climbing permit.

We ran into more trouble almost as soon as we got on the mountain when Scott fell into a crevasse. I stopped the fall, but not before his shoulder popped out of its socket. Eventually, Scott healed well enough to climb again and we started going high. Our progress was halted when we got avalanched below Camp IV while going to the aid of French climber Chantal Mauduit, who had summitted but was having trouble getting down. Scott and I were lucky to survive the avalanche, but decided not to give up. We made one final attempt on the summit, after almost two months on K2, but got pinned down by bad weather at Camp IV. We were stuck there for three nights before catching a break in the weather just long enough for us to summit. As we climbed higher, we saw we were in for a dicey descent when huge clouds rolled in. During the entire upper part of the climb, I had questioned whether we should continue, and now I was certain we had made a mistake by not turning back. We eventually made it safely back to high camp, but our problems weren't over. An incapacitated climber, Gary Ball, needed help getting down to Base Camp through a full-on storm. It was an epic climb and an epic descent.

CAMP IV ON K2 *26,000 feet | 7,930 meters* At 26,000 feet, just below the final summit pyramid on the Abruzzi Ridge route, this tiny tent was our shelter and staging point for our summit assault. Scott Fischer and I had to dig a ledge out of the slope to establish this, our final camp. The weather pinned us down for three days. At extreme altitudes, it is a struggle to exist. Appetites and motivation dwindle. Above 23,000 feet you are in the Death Zone, a place where your body is slowly consuming itself.

SHOULDER OF K2
25,500 feet | 7,777 meters

(PRECEDING PAGES) Scott Fischer and I were making our way toward Camp IV on the Abruzzi Ridge of K2 when we stopped to rest. From this vantage, we got our first glimpse of the upper summit slopes, which had been hidden from view by the ridge itself. To the left is Broad Peak, with a lenticular cloud forming over its three summits—a prelude to another one of the many storms endured during our ten weeks of climbing. The stick to Scott's right is a three-foot bamboo marker with red tape, used to mark our trail so that in bad weather we would be able to find our way down the featureless slopes. Four days later, after our summit, these wands led us to safety in zero-visibility conditions. There had been so much new snow that only the top two inches remained above the surface.

K2 SUMMIT
28,250 feet | 8,611 meters

(OPPOSITE) August 16, 1992, right at noon, Scott Fischer and I stood on the summit of K2 bear hugging each other. We had made good time, but more than that, we were incredibly happy and even relieved just to have made it. K2 is a tough mountain and we thought that climbing it on our first expedition was a great achievement. In fact, we were lucky to have been on the mountain at all: Preparing for the expedition to K2 had become a winter of anguish, one of great disappointments; at one point we weren't sure we'd even have enough money to go. Scott and I made a very strong climbing partnership, so our success was well deserved, we thought. Charlie Mace, who took the photo, had joined us about halfway up on summit day and had climbed the rest of the way with us.

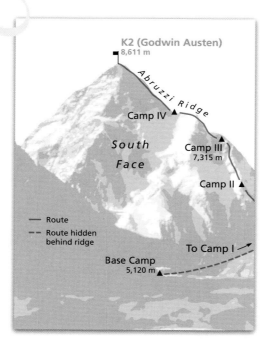

K2 (Godwin Austen)
8,611 m

Abruzzi Ridge

Camp IV

South Face

Camp III
7,315 m

Camp II

—— Route
- - - Route hidden behind ridge

To Camp I

Base Camp
5,120 m

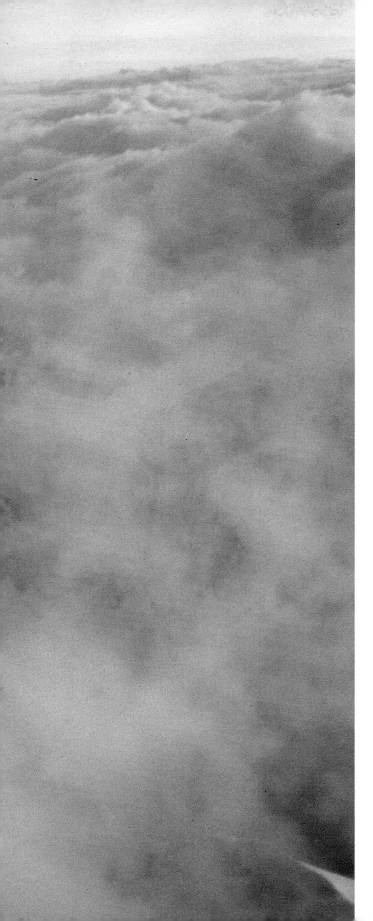

Cold Dawn on K2

27,000 feet | 8,235 meters

Scott Fischer and I have just emerged from the
Bottleneck Couloir after climbing, in the dark,
since 1 a.m. We were already halfway into our
summit bid on this treacherous 8,000-meter peak.
This shot conveys the etherealness of high altitude
and captures the cold and mist as the sun just
emerges. Temperatures are subzero at this point,
and the only way to keep warm is to keep moving.
Taking a photo in freezing conditions like this
while standing on tenuous footing is difficult, to
say the least, and it often results in an off-balance,
one-handed shot. Freezing conditions can also
create problems, as seen here, where a frosted
lens adds to the softness of the image.

CHAPTER FIVE

SHISHAPANGMA | EVEREST NORTH FACE

I N THE SPRING OF 1993, I GUIDED A CLIMB ON PUMORI FOR HALL WENDEL. IT'S not an 8,000-meter peak, but anybody who has made the trek to Everest knows Pumori, a striking peak that makes a lasting impression when you see it. It was fun being by ourselves on the small, moderately technical peak, while looking down at the teeming masses at Everest Base Camp.

Immediately after my descent from Pumori that spring, I traveled with Eric Simonson to Tibet for an attempt on Shishapangma. Simonson was guiding and invited me along; he needed the experience I could provide and knew that I wanted to climb Shishapangma. Alone, I got as high as the Central Summit of the sprawling mountain, less than 20 vertical feet below the 26,286-foot Main Summit. But the snow conditions were unsafe for the final ridge traverse, so I turned around.

For autumn, I had hopes of making a three-day unsupported ascent of Everest's North Face. I had admired Reinhold Messner's solo ascent and I really wanted to test myself by climbing solo. I was interested in the physical and psychological aspects of being completely alone on Everest. But the weather during that season never became stable enough for me to achieve my goal of a solo ascent. After five attempts on the North Face were aborted due to avalanche, I turned in desperation to the North Ridge—the route of my first ascent in 1990. I made two further attempts, but by then it was late autumn and it was way too cold and way too windy.

AMA DABLAM   *14,000 feet | 4,270 meters* **While at Ama Dablam Base Camp in 1993, I noticed the very calm and soothing view as the clouds parted to give a glimpse of the upper portion of Ama Dablam. The peak was just beginning to emerge above the small cairn, which echoes the shape of the mountain. Ama Dablam holds special meaning for the Sherpa. This image brings to mind the spiritual aspects of Himalayan climbing and the things I've learned from the Sherpa and their Buddhist ways.**

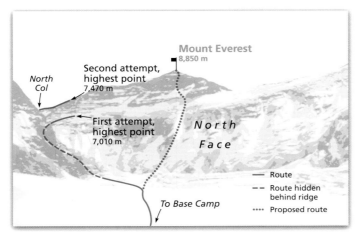

Shishapangma

Central Summit ■ 8,012 m

N.E. Ridge

Camp IV
7,440 m

Camp III

*To Camp I,
Base Camp*

Camp II
6,700 m

— Route
-- Route hidden
behind ridge

Mount Everest
■ 8,850 m

*North
Col*

Second attempt,
highest point
7,470 m

First attempt,
highest point
7,010 m

*North
Face*

To Base Camp

— Route
-- Route hidden
behind ridge
···· Proposed route

PUMORI

20,000 feet | 6,100 meters

(PRECEDING PAGES) Pumori is very close to Everest, and while climbing high on our route in the spring of 1993, we could see Everest's Base Camp teeming with dozens of tents and hundreds of people. The busy scene down there was in stark contrast to our small endeavor, four climbers making an attempt on Pumori, just a group of friends on what amounts to a minor peak in the Himalaya. At night, for fun, we would signal climbers on Everest by flashing our headlamps, and they would flash us back. I've always liked this photo because of its simplicity and the dramatic splash of color—one of our Sherpa team members coming up the ridge, amid a field of icy whites and blues. Ama Dablam is the prominent peak on the right.

EVEREST NORTH FACE

25,000 feet | 7,625 meters

(OPPOSITE) Intrigued by the physical and psychological aspects of being completely alone on Everest, I chose to climb solo. This is a self-portrait taken high on the North Ridge. The shadow of my ski pole, with my camera attached at the top, can be seen in the foreground. Five attempts on the North Face were turned back by avalanche dangers, and another attempt on the North Ridge also failed. I finally turned back at 25,000 feet because high winds made climbing higher impossible.

CHAPTER SIX

EVEREST SOUTH COL | LHOTSE | CHO OYU

I KICKED OFF ONE OF MY MOST SUCCESSFUL YEARS, IN TERMS OF CLIMBING BIG MOUN-tains, on Everest with Rob Hall, whom I had met on K2. Rob had guided Everest before for his company and he asked me to guide with him in 1994. We had six phenomenal clients, all strong, motivated, and experienced. Rob and I just pointed them in the right direction and we all climbed together to the summit. That fabulous climb proved how successful a guided ascent of the mountain can be.

I thought we had done good work, but I still wanted more. I had suggested to Rob earlier that we do Lhotse as well. The idea made a lot of sense because Lhotse is right there—you climb from the same Base Camp. Already acclimatized after Everest, we climbed Lhotse in three days. We had been on the summit of Everest seven days earlier, and had descended, rested at Base Camp for two days, and then made our Alpine-style climb of Lhotse. The upper part of the route on Lhotse is a long snow couloir that gets quite steep higher up. Using the front points of our crampons, with two ice tools each, we made a very rapid and direct ascent of the peak. That was the first tandem climb Rob and I ever did, and it proved our con-cept would work: Climb one 8,000-meter peak; then, already acclimated, make a fast-and-light, Alpine-style attempt on a second 8,000-meter peak.

That autumn we returned to Nepal for Cho Oyu, the sixth highest peak. We got to the summit of the 26,905-foot peak, a fitting conclusion to an amazing year.

KHUMBU ICEFALL   *20,000 feet | 6,100 meters* A climber negotiates this unusual ladder rig to sur-mount a sheer ice wall in the heart of the Khumbu Icefall on Mount Everest in 1995. Nine ladder sections were lashed together to ascend this 50-foot serac face. Guy ropes are anchored to each side to keep the rig stable. These ladder sections are carried into the Icefall and placed by a group of Sherpa climbers known as the "Icefall Sherpa," who figure out where the ladders and fixed lines need to go.

WESTERN CWM

21,000 feet | 6,405 meters

(PRECEDING PAGES) In the Western Cwm below Camp I, heavily crevassed areas of the Khumbu Glacier soon give way to the chaos of the Khumbu Icefall as the glacier tumbles downhill. I was just above the Icefall when I took this photograph. It shows a part of the route where the breakup starts big time if you're going downhill. If you're going uphill, you have to weave and wind through a maze of crevasses until you are above the heavily broken section of the glacier and reach Camp I at about 21,000 feet.

CHO OYU

21,000 feet | 6,405 meters

(OPPOSITE) The route toward the upper camps is clearly defined by the trail of footprints in the early morning light on the Northwest Ridge of Cho Oyu, our Camp I visible at 21,000 feet. Rob Hall and I guided this peak together for the first time in 1994. Earlier that year, we had successfully climbed Everest and Lhotse in succession. In autumn, we climbed the sixth highest peak in the world. At 26,905 feet, Cho Oyu is considered one of the technically easiest of the 8,000-meter peaks. Because of that, it is the second busiest of the commercially guided big mountains and offers a relatively high rate of success.

Mount Everest
8,850 m

South Col

Lhotse
8,501 m

Camp IV
7,925 m

Lhotse Camp II
7,865 m

Camp III

Everest Camp II
Lhotse Camp I
6,400 m

Camp I

— Route

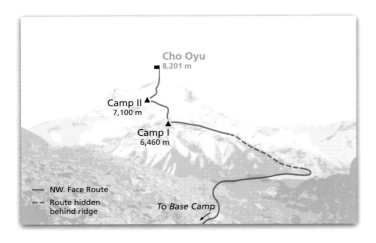

Cho Oyu
8,201 m

Camp II
7,100 m

Camp I
6,460 m

— NW. Face Route
-- Route hidden behind ridge

To Base Camp

LHOTSE SUMMIT
27,890 feet | 8,501 meters

(PRECEDING PAGES) Rob Hall took this shot of me approaching the precarious, wafer-thin summit of Lhotse. Behind me are the upper reaches of Everest, a perspective that can only be seen from Lhotse, where few climbers venture. Rob captured the exposed nature of climbing on Lhotse, as well as this wonderful angle on the upper 3,000 feet of Everest.

EVEREST
19,000 feet | 5,795 meters

(BELOW) Rob Hall and I—immediately after climbing out of the Khumbu Icefall following our three-day ascent of Lhotse—were met by our sirdar, Ang Tshering, with beers and a big smile, and then he took this picture. This spring was the beginning of a great friendship and partnership between Rob and me—and the beginning of a spectacularly successful season. In the autumn we went to Cho Oyu. The next year we went to Everest, Makalu, Gasherbrum I, and Gasherbrum II. I also went to New Zealand and climbed Mount Cook with Rob. The two of us became exceptionally close friends, which made what happened on Everest in 1996 incredibly painful.

EVEREST GROUP

(OPPOSITE) This is the classic shot of the Everest group: The triumvirate of Everest, Lhotse, and Nuptse seen from high on neighboring Pumori. This grouping is often called the Horseshoe, and it arguably is the greatest mountain cirque in the world. The Khumbu Glacier contained within this valley—known as the Western Cwm—is the route most frequently taken to the summit of Everest from the Nepal or south side. This route was the pioneering ascent route on Everest, climbed during the peak's first summit in 1953 by Edmund Hillary and Tenzing Norgay. Climbing on Pumori is a good place to be if for no other reason than to get this perfect angle on the architecture of Everest.

CHAPTER SEVEN

EVEREST SOUTH COL | MAKALU
GASHERBRUM I | GASHERBRUM II

IN 1995, MY CLIMBING SEASON BEGAN WHEN ROB HALL AND I WENT BACK TO Everest to guide six clients. We were joined by guide Guy Cotter, and everyone used oxygen. I make it a point to use supplemental oxygen each time I guide on Everest because I am there to ensure the safety of my clients. Our group reached the South Summit, but difficult snow conditions and extreme winds turned us back a disappointing 300 feet short of the summit.

After the attempt on Everest, I went to Makalu for a lightweight attempt with Rob Hall and Veikka Gustafsson. Rob and I, already acclimatized from Everest, and Veikka, from his climb of Lhotse, were in excellent condition. We had enough experience to feel comfortable with our abilities to manage the terrain on our own, so we climbed unroped for speed. The knife-edge summit was so narrow that the only way for all three of us to fit was to straddle it like a horse.

I returned home to the United States for two weeks after Makalu before traveling to Pakistan, where again I met Rob Hall. We set off trekking along the Baltoro. Still acclimatized from Everest and Makalu, we first climbed Gasherbrum II in a four-day Alpine-style ascent. At our high camp, Rob decided not to continue, so I climbed to the summit alone. We rested a couple of days, and then I did Gasherbrum I in a 30-hour push from Base Camp. Rob had gone home, so I was climbing with Carlos Carsolio and two Polish climbers. We reached the top on July 15.

EVEREST SOUTHEAST RIDGE *28,000 feet | 8,540 meters* The upper part of the Southeast Ridge route ascends to the summit from the South Col. A couple of climbers can barely be seen farther down the ridge, approaching the feature known as the Balcony, basically halfway from the South Col to the summit. Once beyond that point, climbers ascend the Southeast Ridge proper. Makalu is the peak in the background. Ten days after this picture was taken, we were on the summit of Makalu, looking back at Everest.

MAKALU SUMMIT
27,824 feet | 8,481 meters

(PRECEDING PAGES) Veikka Gustafsson and I crowded for a spot on the summit of Makalu, literally straddling the ridge, while Rob Hall took this photograph. Shortly after this, Rob joined us on the tiny summit. Then there were three of us sitting there like three kids astride a big horse, our feet draped over each side. From the top we could look down the West Face and see all the way to the colored specks of our tents at Base Camp, 14,000 feet below, where my girlfriend, Paula, and Rob Hall's wife, Jan, were waiting for us. We spent only a few minutes on top before making our way back down. We descended quickly, and that day we reached Camp II. The following day we were safely back at Base Camp in the company of our loved ones.

SOUTHEAST RIDGE
28,700 feet | 8,753 meters

(OPPOSITE) Rob Hall nears our turn-around point at the South Summit of Everest during our expedition; Makalu is centered in the distance. We had six clients that year. We all used oxygen, and we were constantly in radio communication as well. Guiding requires a very different approach to climbing; I am there is to ensure the safety of my clients. There's no room for a personal agenda when you are guiding. We turned around here when confronted with bad snow conditions and extreme winds. There's no denying that it is a great disappointment to stop just 300 feet short of the summit of Everest, but that's just the way it works sometimes. No summit is worth dying for.

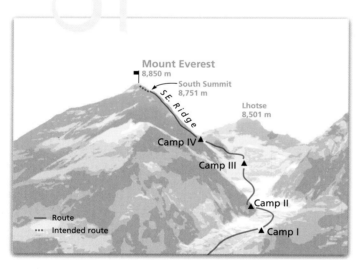

Mount Everest
8,850 m
South Summit
8,751 m
S.E. Ridge
Lhotse
8,501 m
Camp IV
Camp III
Camp II
Camp I
— Route
··· Intended route

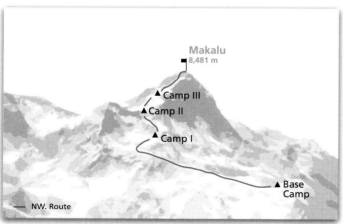

Makalu
8,481 m
Camp III
Camp II
Camp I
Base Camp
— NW. Route

FOOTPRINTS TO GASHERBRUM II
26,361 feet | 8,035 meters

A trail of footprints marks my passage along
the final ridge to the top of Gasherbrum II. I was
very close to the summit when I took this picture.
My ski pole was back at the crest of the ridge,
left behind to mark where I wanted to begin the
descent down the face. Rob Hall had climbed up
with me, but he had turned around a few hours
before I took this photograph. He was not feeling
well and said he would be waiting for me back at
Camp IV. Alone now, and high on an 8,000-meter
peak, I took care to be conservative and make
smart decisions. A minor mishap could lead to
catastrophe because, given my position, no one
would be able to assist. That is why I left my ski
pole to mark my descent. For me, the feeling of
being alone on top of one of the highest peaks
in the world is intoxicating. Added to that is the
sense of extreme isolation and solitude, which was
emphasized by that lonely line of footprints.

CATHEDRAL PEAKS

(Opposite) The Cathedral Peaks are examples of the tremendous variety of stunning mountains that one walks past on the way toward the larger peaks—K2, Broad Peak, Gasherbrum I, and Gasherbrum II—farther up the Baltoro Glacier. The more famous landmark, Trango Tower, is off to the left, and the tower of Uli Biaho is farther down the valley. The walls of these peaks are sheer and the rock for the most part is solid, so they make for incredibly demanding big walls at high altitude. I found it amazing that on my way to an 8,000-meter mountain, I passed these challenging rock-climbing peaks that are quite high in their own right. I can't help but think that there is endless potential for climbing here.

MAKALU SUMMIT RIDGE

27,824 feet | 8,481 meters

(Following Pages) Rob Hall takes the final steps to the summit of Makalu as he carefully traverses the corniced ridge. Veikka Gustafsson and I have already reached the tiny summit, a knife-edge ridge, and we're waiting for Rob to join us. Rob has to stay well below the ridge crest, well beneath the possible fracture line that could appear if the cornices should break free of the ridge, or he would be in mortal danger. This was an immensely enjoyable climb, with perfect conditions, close and person-able companions, and a good result: four days up, one day down.

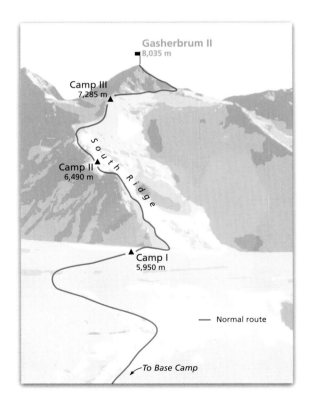

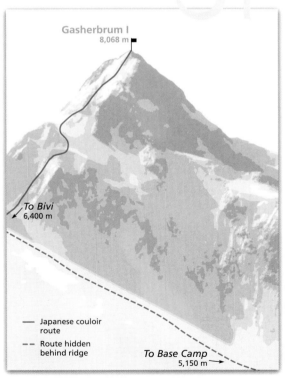

CHAPTER EIGHT

EVEREST SOUTH COL | BROAD PEAK

THE SPRING SEASON OF 1996 ON EVEREST IS INFAMOUS. I WAS CLIMBING LEADER of the IMAX Filming Expedition, responsible for all the food and equipment and other gear, while David Breashears was in charge of the filming. To try to make a film, particularly with the enormous IMAX camera, made climbing arduous. When the storm of May 10 took the lives of good friends Scott Fischer and Rob Hall, we were faced with the tough decision of whether to stay and finish the project or return home. We decided to stay, and on May 23 the perseverance of our team paid off. In the autumn, I guided an ascent of Cho Oyo on behalf of Rob's guide service; his former guides were pitching in to maintain his business.

In the spring of 1997, I was back on Mount Everest with a film crew, this time for a NOVA program. Our team started from the South Col at ten o'clock at night to provide a margin of safety from the crowds we feared: Too many people on the final ridge would make the ascent dangerous. Feeling psychological strength in numbers, and a little summit fever, the majority often follow the lead of a few. Higher up, especially on the summit ridge, too many people present a bottleneck at crucial choke points, such as the Hillary Step. That fact was proven during the spring of 1996, when climbers were delayed on the way up and on the way down.

After Everest, I went to the Karakoram to attempt Broad Peak with Veikka Gustafsson. Both of us acclimatized from Everest, we climbed it with just two camps.

EVEREST SUMMIT DAY   *29,035 feet | 8,850 meters*   Our summit day during the tragic and now famous season of 1996 was the conclusion of a very trying expedition. The day was spectacular, a summit day of dreams, perfectly calm and clear. The snow was quite deep; almost two weeks had passed since someone had walked these slopes. Five hundred feet below me on the summit, the rest of the team gathered at the Balcony. Sunlight was playing on Makalu, the prominent peak, and Kanchenjunga, on the far left.

SEA OF BOTTLES

26,000 feet | 7,930 meters

(PRECEDING PAGES) Hundreds of empty oxygen bottles lie strewn across the rocks of the South Col at 26,000 feet on Mount Everest, the site of Camp IV, accumulating since the first attempts on route in the 1950s. In recent years, however, the pile has been shrinking. Hundreds of thousands of dollars have been raised for the cleanup of this site. Also, early in the 1990s, Rob Hall and other guides began offering a bonus, from their own funds, for Sherpa to carry bottles down from the col. The idea was that after carrying a load of equipment to Camp IV, the Sherpa would return down the mountain not with empty packs, but with discarded oxygen bottles instead.

ALONE ON THE SUMMIT

29,035 feet | 8,850 meters

(OPPOSITE) This portrait at the summit of Everest was taken at 11 a.m., May 23, 1996, after a 12-hour ascent alone. I was atop Mount Everest for the fourth time, but this ascent was very different from the previous summits: The IMAX project was so all-consuming, and the tragic events of May 10 so devastating, that this summit had a feel altogether different from previous climbs. I felt hugely relieved that we would accomplish what we set out to do: get a 42-pound IMAX camera to the summit. After all that had happened, I also felt a tremendous sense of relief that I had not let anybody down. I reached the summit before the others and waited there about half an hour before David Breashears, who took this photo, caught up to me on top.

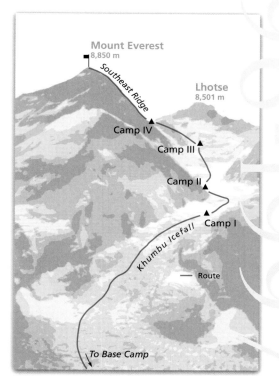

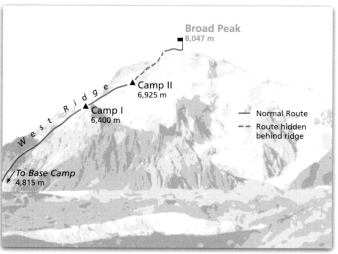

THE YELLOW BAND
25,000 feet | 7,625 meters

The Yellow Band at 25,000 feet on the Lhotse Face
en route to the South Col from the Western Cwm
is an obvious band of sandstone, a very distinct
feature that lies exposed on most sides of Everest.
Every climber must ascend through this layer,
which can present unexpected difficulties. The
Band can be a little tricky: After climbing the
Lhotse Face you've got to scramble up and over the
rock band, then keep going up the final slopes to
the South Col, more than 3,000 feet to the summit.
This image shows the Southwest Face and the
upper part of the West Ridge. An interesting geo-
logical fact is that the Yellow Band was once below
the sea. But the action of plate tectonics caused the
massive uplifting of the Himalaya when the Indian
subcontinent crashed into Asia. The Himalaya are
still growing at "about the rate your fingernails
grow," according to acclaimed mountain geogra-
pher Brad Washburn.

BREASHEARS IN ACTION
25,000 feet | 7,625 meters

(OPPOSITE) The incomparable David Breashears films at 25,000 feet on the steep slopes of the Lhotse Face during our Everest IMAX expedition. A visionary director and accomplished climber, he was the perfect choice to make this film at high altitude. His rule was never get ahead of the camera, because if David saw something that made him decide, "I'm going to shoot a scene here," you had to be close by, real close. When David stopped to set up that big camera, he might say, "Ed, you know, you walk ahead. I'm going to film you." And if I had let myself drift way ahead, I'd have to come all the way back, and that would be a lot of extra work and an intolerable delay.

BREASHEARS AND CAMERA
25,000 feet | 7,625 meters

(BELOW) David Breashears reloads the IMAX camera bare-handed in frigid conditions. Fearful of getting lint on the inner mechanics of the camera, David was adamant about removing his gloves and glove liners while loading film. He was talented enough not only to climb Everest but also to focus beyond the climbing difficulties to do the filming. At elevations where most people are barely able to put their shoes on, David was performing the complex duties of filmmaker. He had redesigned the IMAX camera to make it functional on Everest. Committed to making the film, he spent two years with the Imax Corporation redesigning the camera to make it lighter.

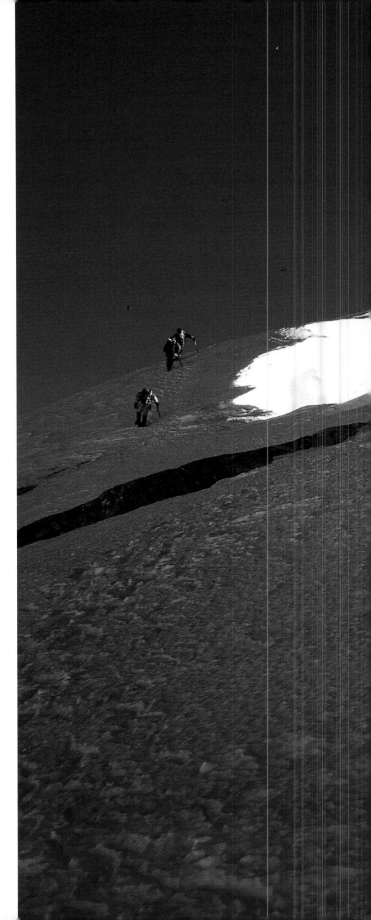

TENUOUS TRAVERSE

(PRECEDING PAGES) I took this photo in 1997 on my last ascent of Everest. Standing at the base of the Hillary Step, I looked back to see other climbers following the narrow Southeast Ridge from the South Summit (the sunlit dome just behind the last climber). The image shows how steep and exposed the final ridge is. In some places it is so thin you can see air through the hole left behind by your ice ax— an indication that perhaps you were too close to the crest of the corniced ridge. A fixed rope ensures the safety of climbers making this traverse, because there are long, steep drop-offs on either side. I was back on the mountain again with David Breashears the year after the IMAX filming, this time for a NOVA program. We were on the upper slopes of Everest just after sunrise. By any measure, that is very early to be this high, and our reward was a beautiful sunrise.

THE FINAL STEPS

29,000 feet | 8,845 meters

(RIGHT) Three climbers take the last steps to the summit of Everest. Once the final cornice is sur-mounted, there are only several dozen steps left to reach the top of the world. Great care must be taken to stay far to the side of these overhanging cornices, as the drop-off down the East Face (to the right) is quite sheer and treacherous. In bad weather, climbers have disappeared over this precipice, often while descending, not being able to discern the cornice edge from the sky beneath their feet. I took this photo very early, approximately 6:30 a.m. The sun is still quite low on the horizon to the right, and therefore the cornices are lit from the side and below, which made for an unusual composition. Together with my client, David Carter, David Breashears, Pete Athans, Guy Cotter, and I reached the summit at 6:45 a.m. It was my fifth summit on Everest and my earliest time yet to reach the top.

RELAXATION

(BELOW) After two and a half months on Everest, a terrible time of pressure and tragedy and uncertainty, I sit with three extraordinary teammates—my wife Paula, Araceli Segarra, and David Breashears—on the steps of a teahouse in Deboche, the first real village we encountered on our way home from the mountain. For the first time in months, we could relax. Until then, we had hundreds of details to consider each day, schedules to keep, hazards to avoid, danger and trouble beyond our control, delays, frustrations, and pressures. On top of that was the tragedy of May 10, during which I lost two close personal friends, Rob Hall and Scott Fischer, high on the mountain. It had been a difficult time. But now we could at last rest, make future plans, and enjoy the warmth of an oncoming summer.

HILLARY STEP
28,700 feet | 8,750 meters

(OPPOSITE) Several climbers make the traverse along the knife-edge Southeast Ridge, from the South Summit of Everest. Three climbers can be seen just above the Hillary Step; the lowest one has just surmounted this last of the major technical difficulties en route to the summit. At an elevation of 28,700 feet, the storied Hillary Step can present a daunting obstacle: 40 feet of near-vertical rock climbing. The step is draped with a number of old fixed ropes. These can be friable due to deterioration from exposure to weather and sunlight. Typically, a new rope to aid the ascent and descent is fixed by the first team going up each season. Once above the step, climbers have to be careful not to stray too far out on the corniced ridgelines, as the wind-blown snow can collapse at any time.

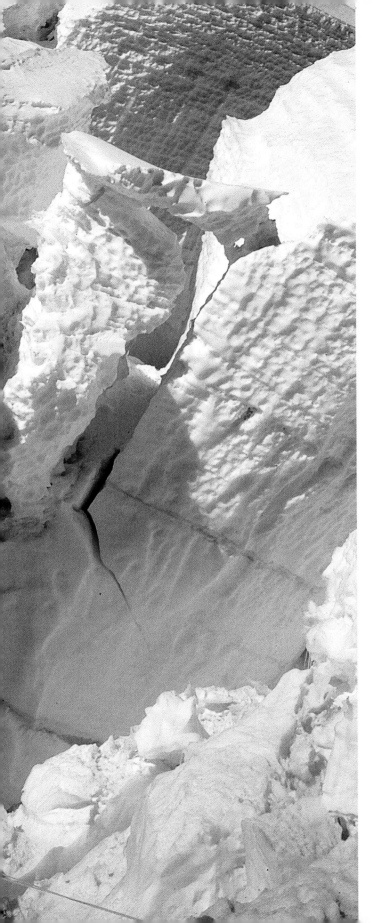

THE WESTERN CWM
21,000 feet | 6,405 meters

(PRECEDING PAGES) The immensity of the Western Cwm is depicted in this shot, which shows the entire length of the Cwm from the top of the Icefall to the Lhotse Face, which is some three miles distant. The West Shoulder of Everest comes down from the left and the ridge of Nuptse comes down from the right, with Lhotse straight ahead. I took this photo from just above the Khumbu Icefall. The last crevasse of the Icefall is visible here, with a group of Sherpa heading for Camp I just up the valley.

KHUMBU GYMNASTICS
20,000 feet | 6,100 meters

(LEFT) A Sherpa works in the Khumbu Icefall. Day in and day out these loyal team members carry heavy loads over the difficult and often treacherous terrain of the Icefall, one of the most dangerous parts of the route to the summit of Everest from the Nepal side. Ladders, fixed lines, and other aids make it possible for Sherpa and Western climbers to move through the chaos of ever shifting ice blocks called seracs, formed when the Khumbu Glacier tumbles steeply downhill. The Sherpa climbers are well trained and very experienced in these maneuvers, but their obvious strength seems beyond comprehension. On a typical day, Sherpa in support of an expedition will leave Base Camp at 2 a.m. to quickly negotiate the Icefall during the coldest and therefore safest, most stable part of the day. They deposit their loads at Camp I and return to Base Camp for breakfast. Their work for the day complete, the Sherpa relax and prepare to do it again the next day—and again and again and again.

EVEREST CAMP IV

26,000 feet | 7,930 meters

(OPPOSITE) The South Col is actually the saddle between Everest and the neighboring peak of Lhotse, a "pass" big and flat enough to accommodate tents, oxygen, and other supplies for climbers making an attempt on the summit, still more than 3,000 feet above. The altitude alone is debilitating, and people tend to move about in a zombie-like fashion. An average of only two nights are spent at this camp during an expedition: the night before the summit attempt and the night just after. Conditions are so severe that additional time spent here is more debilitating than restful. The route from the Col to the summit can be seen in this image: along the snow-covered rocks to the Triangular Face, then up to the Balcony, and on to the Southeast Ridge.

TRAFFIC ON LHOTSE

25,000 feet | 7,625 meters

(BELOW) As I crossed the Yellow Band at 25,000 feet on the Lhotse Face in 1997, I looked down to see nearly 40 climbers following up the fixed rope toward Camp IV. A common scenario on Everest, especially when the weather in May continues to be fickle, is that teams tend to stack up and wait for a few of the stronger climbing teams to make the decision to go for the summit.

SHADOW OF EVEREST

28,500 feet | 8,690 meters

(FOLLOWING PAGES) Early on May 23, 1997, from 28,500 feet on Everest, I witnessed the incredible shadow of the mountain forming to the west as the sun rose behind me. The full moon from the night before was still visible. The bluish cast of the high atmosphere can also be seen.

CHAPTER NINE

MANASLU | DHAULAGIRI

VEIKKA GUSTAFSSON AND I HAD BEEN TURNED BACK ON DHAULAGIRI in 1998, so we decided to go for another try and also to attempt Manaslu. This would be one of my most enjoyable expeditions to the Himalaya, just me and Veikka and Dorje, our sirdar and cook. The approach was through one of the most remote parts of Nepal, and Veikka and I were constantly amazed at both the openness of the culture and how quickly a rapport is established between strangers. Dorje would ask a farmer for permission to use his fire to cook, and we would spend some time in the house with the family. We would sleep in the barn or a nearby shed or tent. It was a fabulous way to experience the Himalaya.

Manaslu is off the beaten path, in a part of the range that still has a wilderness feel, both on the approach and on the mountain. Although the route had been climbed before, it was not well known to us, so we had to figure it out ourselves and detour around some objective dangers. We spent a total of 14 days on the peak. Our final day was cold and windy, but the summit was wild and beautiful.

After Manaslu, we trekked down to a nearby village. A helicopter met us there and took us to Dhaulagiri Base Camp, which saved us weeks of trekking and helped preserve our acclimatization. We lucked out and had good weather and good conditions; we were able to climb Dhaulagiri Alpine style in just three days.

MANASLU SUMMIT *26,781 feet | 8,163 meters* Finnish climber Veikka Gustafsson stands on the summit of Manaslu in 1999. Rocky, snow-covered towers are characteristic of Manaslu. We spent 14 days on the mountain, gradually moving up, figuring out the route, and acclimatizing. We placed a total of three camps above our Base Camp before reaching the top. Our summit day was a good one for climbing high.

WAVES OF PEAKS, MANASLU

17,000 feet | 5,185 meters

(PRECEDING PAGES) The low morning sun, as seen from high on Manaslu, silhouettes the Himalaya southeast of the mountain. Veikka Gustafsson and I already were quite high on the mountain and the sun has just come up behind us. There had been no rain for months; 1999 was one of the driest years in the Himalaya in memory. With so little snow, my friend Eric Simonson—with whom I first attempted Everest in 1987— and his team were able to find George Mallory's body on Everest while we were on Manaslu. Layers of smoke from villages and forest fires are visible in the photo. It seemed to us that the air was not moving at all— no wind, no rain—which made for phenomenal climbing conditions.

HIGH CAMP ON MANASLU

24,700 feet | 7,530 meters

(OPPOSITE) Veikka Gustafsson is just approaching our third and highest camp on Manaslu, which is among the most remote camps I've ever had in the Himalaya. It was a very lonely little camp that we set up the day before our summit push. But it was home and our specially made bivvy tent was lightweight and comfortable. As we descended from the summit, we were amazed to see another tent. Two Spanish climbers had followed our steps and placed their camp next to ours. With all the space around our tent, it was humorous that these guys camped right on top of us. But at that altitude, there's a feeling of safety in numbers, a sense of comfort that comes from being close to others.

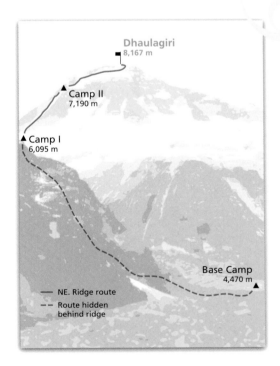

Dhaulagiri
8,167 m

▲ Camp II
7,190 m

▲ Camp I
6,095 m

Base Camp
4,470 m ▲

— NE. Ridge route
-- Route hidden behind ridge

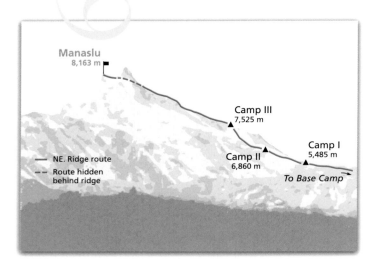

Manaslu
8,163 m

Camp III
7,525 m

Camp II
6,860 m

Camp I
5,485 m

—— NE. Ridge route
- - Route hidden
behind ridge

To Base Camp

MANASLU PORTERS

16,000 feet | 4,880 meters

(PRECEDING PAGES) Porters from the village of Soma Gon carry equipment during the last day of our approach trek to Manaslu in 1999. This is a remote part of Nepal, far off the usual trekking routes. We had employed lowland Nepalese porters for the first several days while traveling toward Manaslu, but at Soma Gon our sirdar, Dorje, told us we had to release the porters and hire local villagers. This rule had become established in this village, and so we abided by it.

TIBETAN BOY

(OPPOSITE) Manaslu lies very close to the Nepalese border with Tibet. The last village before Base Camp is Soma Gon, where Tibetan refugees have made their home. This is a politically sensitive region and we needed special visas to travel in the area because it was so accessible to the Tibetan frontier. The boy holds a prayer flag, which is attached vertically to a tall pole. Tibetan-based villages can be differentiated by these telltale symbols of the Buddhist faith, whereas lowland Nepalese are often Hindu.

DHAULAGIRI, ABOVE CAMP I
(PRECEDING PAGES) Veikka Gustafsson travels from Camp I to our final camp on Dhaulagiri. We were climbing Alpine style and that can make for a pack between 40 and 45 pounds, but it's a wonderful way to climb. We were able to do it because we had just spent two weeks on Manaslu and so were already accustomed to the thin air at altitude. Veikka and I are well matched in temperament and ability, and it felt great to be up there going fast and light. I love the wild feel of this photo, a feeling that was emphasized by the fact that the two of us had Dhaulagiri entirely to ourselves.

MANASLU
21,000 feet | 6,405 meters
(OPPOSITE) On Manaslu we encountered a little icefall that we had to negotiate before we could gain a key ridge. This photo shows me climbing up toward the ridge. Veikka and I shared the work on this climb by taking turns breaking trail in half-hour intervals. Veikka took this photo as I climbed up in his steps to take over the lead.

LIGHTWEIGHT CAMP ON DHAULAGIRI
23,500 feet | 7,170 meters
(BELOW) When Veikka and I are trying to climb a mountain in a single push, we don't take sleeping bags. Instead, we take a down quilt that was made especially for us. We also sleep in our down suits, so it's an integrated sleeping system: We use the down suits, which we have to carry anyway, to save weight on sleeping bags, which gives us greater versatility for less weight. By squeezing into a tiny tent, we share body heat. It's a very efficient system, and it's quite warm with two of us jammed into close quarters like this.

END OF THE CLIMB, MANASLU

14,000 feet | 4,270 meters

(LEFT) Veikka is packing gear in the sunshine at Base Camp, one of the most comfortable we've ever had, at the end of the Manaslu climb in 1999. The expedition was a huge success. The trek in was fantastic, the route was interesting, and we did really well on the climb itself—three camps and the summit in just 14 days. Dorje, our sirdar, organized a group of porters to take our gear down to a village at about 10,000 feet. We were just about to trek down there as well, where we would get picked up by a helicopter for our trip to Dhaulagiri.

MANASLU, FROM SOMA GON

(FOLLOWING PAGES) The true Summit of Manaslu is on the left; the "summit" on the right is the East Summit. Our route basically followed the right-hand skyline to the plateau, then went behind the East Summit to the saddle, and from there to the summit. Manaslu is a mountain of exceptional beauty. I took this shot from the village of Soma Gon, where many Tibetan refugees have settled.

CHAPTER TEN

ANNAPURNA

I WENT TO ANNAPURNA FOR THE FIRST TIME IN 2000 WITH MICHAEL KENNEDY, Neil Beidleman, and Veikka Gustafsson, a strong team of climbers. I think we were all a little surprised to find the journey to the mountain so difficult, even technical. The northern route was quite circuitous, with almost unbelievable daily elevation gains and sections that were so steep we had to rope up the porters; even they were having a tough time on this approach. It's easy to see why the trip into the north side is not a popular trek like the circuit route: It's simply too arduous.

Once at Base Camp, we basically followed the route up to Camp II that the French pioneered in 1950. We established the camp at about 18,500 feet and spent two nights there. The next day we climbed higher into the basin so that we could see the route options: the Northeast Buttress, the French Route, the Dutch Rib. When we got into the basin we also saw what we were up against: The whole basin is threatened by a series of ice cliffs that totally surround the upper part of the mountain. We watched these things calve off and create huge avalanches. The objective danger was off the scale, and we all knew immediately we had to turn around. Some climbers have gone up from that side, but from our point of view the route was totally untenable. The risks were just too great. We knew we'd have to come back and look for a more sane route to the top.

LONE CLIMBER, ANNAPURNA APPROACH   A team member makes his way up a steep ridge on the approach to the north side of Annapurna. The journey is difficult. In a single day we would descend 2,000 feet, gain 5,000 feet, and then have to descend another 4,000 feet, all on a steep, narrow route with unreal exposure. This approach was pioneered by the French team of 1950, led by Maurice Herzog, the first expedition to summit an 8,000-meter peak.

(PRECEDING PAGES) This looks like a climbing shot taken at high altitude, but it was actually a view on our trek to the north side during the spring season. Annapurna is a huge massif, and in this picture you can see the Northwest Face, which was first climbed by Reinhold Messner. It's difficult and perilous, given the high level of danger from falling ice. The route we proposed to climb is around the corner to the left and out of sight. This photo shows some of the team members trekking through one of the passes we had to cross to reach Base Camp. The prominent peak at the right edge of the photo is known as the Fang.

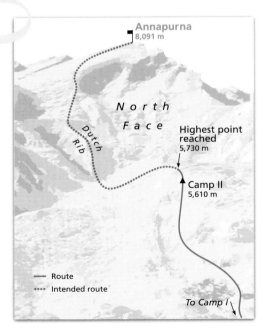

Annapurna
8,091 m

North
Face

Dutch
Rib

Highest point
reached
5,730 m

Camp II
5,610 m

— Route
···· Intended route

To Camp I

ANNAPURNA PORTERS
11,000 feet | 3,355 meters

(OPPOSITE) Following in the footsteps of Maurice Herzog and his 1950 expedition team was part of the allure when I decided to go to Annapurna with three friends—Neil Beidleman, Michael Kennedy, and Veikka Gustafsson— though we planned to attempt a route on the north side of the massive peak, a different route after Camp II than the one climbed by the French. When we made the arduous trek to Base Camp, we wondered how the French had managed it a half century earlier. In this photo, a group of porters arrive at a ridge crest, the southeast aspect of Dhaulagiri prominent in the distance. In 1999, Veikka and I had climbed Dhaulagiri, and seeing it again from this perspective was like seeing an old friend.

WOMAN IN YELLOW

Near Annapurna, a woman sits by her window cleaning a pot. The beautiful yellows of her shirt and the wall of her house captured me. We passed this small village, whose name I don't think we ever found out, on our way to the north side. It's a very isolated route, one that sees hardly any climbers or trekkers because of its difficulty. The scene evokes the simplicity of life in this quiet and friendly country, which is one of the things that has drawn me to Nepal again and again.

CHAPTER ELEVEN

NANGA PARBAT | SHISHAPANGMA

IHAD BEEN TO SHISHAPANGMA IN 1993 BUT WAS TURNED BACK AT THE CENTRAL Summit, less than 20 feet below the true summit. Snow conditions were dangerous, so I elected not to make the final traverse. In 2001, I decided to go back again with Veikka Gustafsson, hoping we'd find better conditions. The final section of the route involves traversing 300 linear feet to gain 10 feet of elevation. That's what I had not done in 1993, and that's what I had come back to do.

Incredibly, on arrival we found that we had the entire mountain to ourselves. Base Camp is at 18,000 feet, and we put in only two higher camps on our climb to the top. Once we had our camps established, Veikka and I did the climb in three days. Eight years after I was turned back on Shishapangma, we lucked into an ideal summit day.

After Shishapangma, Veikka and I turned our attention to Nanga Parbat. We traveled to Pakistan, where Nanga Parbat stands, apart from the other 8,000-meter mountains. Our route began on the Diamir Face, but soon after we arrived, heavy snows began to fall and continued for two weeks. The upper reaches were buried in several feet of freshly fallen snow while Base Camp suffered daily spells of both rain and snow. The weather kept us pinned down. We made a second trip up to Camp I, and that's when I became convinced the upper mountain was so loaded with snow that it would take weeks to return to safe climbing shape. After much thought and discussion with Veikka, I decided to leave the mountain.

CAMP I, SHISHAPANGMA *21,000 feet | 6,405 meters* **This view from Camp I on Shishapangma captures the ground-blizzard type of conditions that are so frequently encountered when climbing in the Himalaya. Veikka Gustafsson and I were already in our tent when I took this shot of two climbers coming up, fighting the wind and cold to reach the safety of shelter.**

SUMMIT DAY ON SHISHAPANGMA

25,000 feet | 7,625 meters

(PRECEDING PAGES) When things go right, you know you're lucky, and when things are perfect, all you can do is be grateful. On our ascent in the spring of 2001, eight years after I had first attempted Shishapangma, we had an ideal summit day. Climbing conditions could not have been better: hard snow, perfect for cramponing, and great weather. Here Veikka Gustafsson poses on our summit day; we're halfway to the top from high camp. In the distance to the northeast are the dry hills of the Tibetan plateau. Most of the climbing on Shishapangma is circuitous, but the final summit ascent is direct and steep.

DESCENT FROM SHISHAPANGMA

23,000 feet | 7,015 meters

(OPPOSITE) One of the best things about going into the Himalaya again and again is that you get to see the mountains in different moods. This photo was taken on the steep part of the summit ridge as we were descending from the top of Shishapangma in late afternoon. We had had a great day, with perfect climbing conditions, and both Veikka and I felt relaxed and strong. As we came down the ridge, we could see the huge plateau where we had placed our high camp and could see our tiny tent in the middle. The shadows and the clouds made this intimidating scene seem almost soft and warm.

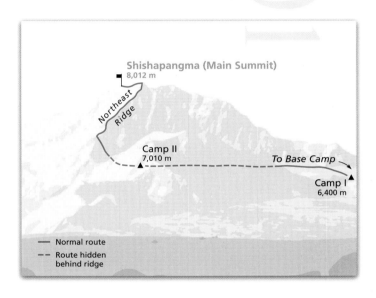

Shishapangma (Main Summit)
8,012 m

Northeast Ridge

Camp II
7,010 m

To Base Camp

Camp I
6,400 m

— Normal route
-- Route hidden behind ridge

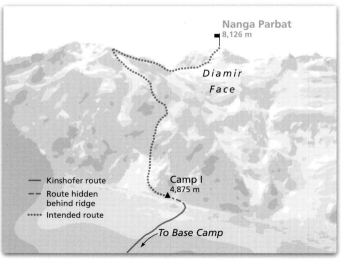

Nanga Parbat
8,126 m

Diamir Face

Camp I
4,875 m

— Kinshofer route
-- Route hidden behind ridge
···· Intended route

To Base Camp

RIDING THE RIDGE, SHISHAPANGMA

26,000 feet | 7,930 meters

Veikka Gustafsson climbs the final ridge between Shishapangma Central and Main Summits. This was near the place where I had turned back in 1993 because of the high potential for avalanche, way beyond what I consider safe for climbing. This time when we got to the Central Summit, the snow conditions were excellent, so Veikka and I set out on the strenuous hour-and-a-half climb along the knife-edge ridge to the Main Summit of the 14th highest mountain on Earth. Mostly our progress consisted of just scooting along, like Veikka is doing in the photo; in some places we were able to grab the ridge crest and kick steps along either side of the ridge. It was quite intimidating because the ridge is steep and very exposed. It's a long way down on either side, so it's not a place to make a mistake. As the photo illustrates, we're not roped up, which is one reason we felt most secure actually sitting and just kind of scooting along the ridge. This is the final section of the route, where you have to traverse 300 linear feet to gain 10 feet of elevation—the only part of the route I had not done in 1993. We reached the summit, spent another hour and a half getting back to this point, and from there raced back to camp.

CHAPTER TWELVE

ANNAPURNA

THE FIRST TIME WE WENT TO ANNAPURNA, IN 2000, THE OBJECTIVE DANGER was off the scale. The upper part of the mountain was completely blocked by ice cliffs. We looked at many different routes, but nothing was acceptable to us. I remained committed to finding a safe route up the peak. In the spring of 2001, French climber Christian Trommsdorff, who knew of what I was trying to do, told me about a route he found on the south side that he thought might offer a way up without the objective dangers faced on the north side.

In spring of 2002, I returned to the mountain with Veikka Gustafsson, Jean Christophe Lafaille, and a group of Basque climbers that included Alberto Inurrategi to see if the route Trommsdorff had been on might go. When we got to Base Camp, we could see that the route held promise but had a trade-off: There was less objective danger, but more time in the Death Zone.

It looked like we might find a safe route to the top until Camp III. Just beyond the camp, a feature called Roc Noir has an 800-foot snow face of about 45°. During the preceding weeks, the winds had deposited a huge amount of snow, and on the day we arrived we found a textbook avalanche slope. For Veikka and myself, the level of risk was unacceptable. Jean Christophe and Alberto chose to continue and they successfully reached the summit a few days later. We were comfortable with our decision. It was a disappointment, to be sure, but we both plan to find another way up.

ANNAPURNA, CAMP I   *17,000 feet I 5,185 meters* Camp I on Annapurna had an incredible location, perched on a glacial ledge almost like a giant balcony, and was also relatively free from avalanche and icefall. From the camp we had a spectacular 360° panoramic view. This photo shows the impressive flank of Annapurna South, but the view from this camp took in the entire South Face of Annapurna, Singu Chuli, and Machapuchare (Fish Tail Peak).

24,000 feet | 7,320 meters

(PRECEDING PAGES) On the impressive East Ridge of Annapurna, our team sets out on an Alpine-style summit push. The two climbers farthest along the ridge are J.-C. Lafaille and Alberto Inurrategi, climbing from Camp III toward Camp IV and, we all hoped, the summit of Annapurna. The climber in the foreground, a member of the Basque team, at that point decided to turn around because he felt the route was too difficult and extended for him to continue. The route follows the corniced section of the East Ridge to the left side of the frame, then climbs steeply up the feature called Roc Noir. Above that, it follows the long, high East Ridge for almost five miles. In the distance are northern Nepal and western Tibet.

MACHAPUCHARE

(OPPOSITE) The popular trek to the Nepalese village known as Annapurna Base Camp lands you about a day below the actual Base Camp used by climbers. This view shows Machapuchare, a prominent landmark in that part of Nepal. The peak is visible from the city of Pokhara, which is the starting point both for the popular trek and for our approach to Annapurna in April. Machapuchare remains a sacred mountain to the Nepalese, so no one can get a permit to climb it. Because of the popularity of trekking in this scenic region of Nepal, we were shocked to see almost no one on our journey in. Tourism was hurt badly in 2002 by geopolitical events, both the fallout from terrorist attacks in the United Sates and an insurgency that year by Maoist rebels in eastern Nepal.

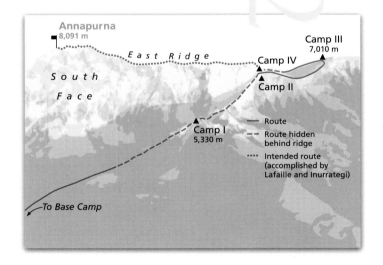

ANNAPURNA CAMP IV
24,500 feet | 7,470 meters

(BELOW) At the end of the long section of corniced ridge, just below Roc Noir, Veikka and I spent the night, much of it deliberating about what to do. We faced an agonizing decision. The route we had selected was high and long but relatively free of objective danger. But at this place it passed a dangerously avalanche-prone slope leading to the point of Roc Noir. By morning, we had come to the unhappy conclusion that the only thing to do was to turn around and go down. Just above the camp pictured here was an 800-foot snow slope leading to the upper East Ridge. The slope presented few climbing difficulties, but it was still very dangerous. Turning back was a tough decision, but you have to have a good feeling about going up, not anguish. Machapuchare is the prominent peak in the distance.

WEST BUTTRESS, SINGU CHULI
18,000 feet | 5,490 meters

(OPPOSITE) A team member begins the ascent of the West Buttress of Singu Chuli above Camp I. This steep and technical feature was the key to reaching the upper slopes of the East Ridge safely, allowing us to avoid the avalanche-prone slopes of the South Face. The East Ridge forms the skyline across the top of this photo. What is shown here is only one section of the long ridge, which was successfully climbed by our partners J.-C. Lafaille and Alberto Inurrategi. Part of the South Face of Annapurna is also visible in the photo. Being on this route gave us renewed appreciation for Dougal Haston's and Don Whillans's climb of the South Face in 1975; it's a long, technically difficult route at high altitude, with some sections vulnerable to avalanche.

CAMP II, ANNAPURNA
20,000 feet | 6,100 meters

(RIGHT) Even though it looks like an entire mountain, this is only the final summit pyramid of the peak—the last few hundred feet of Singu Chuli as seen from Camp II. The West Buttress of this spectacular mountain, the key to our route, comes up to the saddle in the lower right corner of the photograph. From that saddle, we could go on to the East Face and the East Ridge. Our group of four had been on countless Himalayan expeditions, but we agreed that this was one of the most scenic climbs we had ever made.

CAMP II, ANNAPURNA
20,000 feet | 6,100 meters

(FOLLOWING PAGES) Quite often while making this attempt on Annapurna, we encountered afternoon thunderstorms. But, after a while, we got the hang of things, and so we would time our climbing to make sure that during these storms we were in camp and not on a fixed rope or high on a ridge. Every day about 2 p.m. we'd need to be in our tent because we'd be engulfed in the violent, but relatively short, storms. Lightning, snow, and wind would come in suddenly, wail on us for a while, and then dissipate. It was just the nature of climbing in this part of the range. Off the saddle is the top of the West Buttress on Singu Chuli. Annapurna South, one of the many big peaks on the Annapurna massif, is in the distance.

EPILOGUE

ED VIESTURS'S IMAGES IN HIMALAYAN QUEST show not just the ineffable beauty of the world's highest mountains, but how the view has changed for Viesturs himself. Fifteen years ago, a young climber with little more than a strong belief in his own abilities dared to enter the savage arena of the Himalaya. He can now look back over almost unimaginable success.

Viesturs's efforts have, so far, shown him the world from 12 of the highest summits on Earth. Along the way, he has seen both sides of fortune— good luck to survive the rare bad decision made early on, bad luck to meet repeatedly with dangerous conditions on some peaks. The trouble he encountered seemed only to make him stronger and smarter, a better climber; each success served to validate his competence and motivate him further. He survived an aggressive process of natural selection and was transformed from a gung-ho 27-year-old to a wise and accomplished veteran. The difficult but rewarding journey took Viesturs past milestones of joy and heartbreaking tragedy, and a gamut of experiences in between. He is content with what he has done, and from that evolved perspective he looks to fulfill current goals and sees beyond to new kinds of adventures that lie ahead.

Viesturs's growth as a climber is mirrored in his maturation as a human being. Now a 43-year-old father of two children, Viesturs has family commitments that have complicated the logistics of big-league mountaineering. When the children arrived—Gil first, then Ella—his wife, Paula, began staying home instead of going along on the expeditions. And being a parent forced Viesturs to look again at what he does for a living. While always a proponent of smart mountaineering, Viesturs found in his family even greater impetus for a commitment to climbing safely.

What hasn't changed is Viesturs's innate love of mountains, which is what drives him. The fact that he's so good at high-altitude mountaineering he makes it look easy may be a mixed blessing. Each time he ventures into the upper reaches of mountains, among the thin air and ice and rocky spires where human presence is insignificant, he puts his skill and judgment to the most tangible test. Yet it is a place where Ed Viesturs is at home—a place where he has not only survived but also thrived.

Viesturs knows better than anyone that his world is a dangerous place. That he continues to climb is one manifestation of the self-confidence that drew him to the Himalaya. In the upcoming years, Viesturs will return to Nanga Parbat and to Annapurna, undeterred by his lack of success on those peaks in the past. As he prepares logistically for another journey to Pakistan and Nanga Parbat for the spring of 2003, he can see beyond the challenge of the 8,000-meter peaks to a rich life of adventure and family. With his quest drawing toward conclusion, his quiet belief in himself will take him in new directions. For Ed Viesturs, the journey continues.

—PETER POTTERFIELD

BACK IN THE 1980s, ON MY FIRST TRIPS TO THE Himalaya, the hardest part was just getting there, figuring out a way to get invited on an expedition or somehow get the money to pay for the trip. Fifteen years later, after five Everest summits and most of the 8,000-meter peaks, everything is different. I am a veteran of going to the Himalaya and supplying expeditions. That gets easier with experience. These days the hardest part for me is leaving my family and the daily life I have with them. But when I do leave on an expedition, I have to focus totally on the climb—for their sake, and mine. This is what I do.

I look forward to the day when I can have my family with me when I climb. Paula made a number of expeditions with me in the mid-nineties, and it was fantastic. Her presence at Everest Base Camp in 1996 was a tremendous emotional support for me, even though I felt sorrow that she had to suffer through the May 10 tragedy at such close quarters. Paula gave me the strength to persevere when she told me to "climb that mountain like you've never climbed it before."

Now, with Gil and Ella so young, it isn't practical for her to come along. And the kids give me a new sense of responsibility even though I haven't changed my climbing style as a result. I've always been as safe as I can be, or tried to be. But I'll say this: If having kids and being married makes me even more so, I welcome that. Climbing a mountain is irrelevant compared with raising a family and being around to enjoy that.

Some people tell me I climb big mountains so often that the risk increases with each expedition. I disagree. My belief is that the more I go into the mountains the smarter I get, and the safer I get. You learn not to repeat mistakes. If you do it the right way and learn and remember what's happened before, each time you go, you go with more skills.

If my children want to start climbing when they get older, I think it will be great. I'll leave that up to the kids; I'm not going to push them. It won't be too far off—ten years, perhaps—when I may be climbing with Gil, if that is something that appeals to him. A family trip up Mount Rainier sounds like fun; it would bring me back full circle to those days in the early 1980s when I began guiding there. That, really, was the beginning of this whole amazing experience.

I'm planning a return to Nanga Parbat in spring of 2003 and, tentatively, an attempt on Annapurna the following year. Those are the final peaks that stand between me and my goal of climbing the 14 highest mountains. I'm still focused on that. I want to go again to these peaks to look for a way I can climb them safely.

I feel incredibly positive about what I've done. From where I started to where I am now shows that I've lived the dream that I envisioned years ago. To be where I am makes me very happy. When my attempt to stand atop all of the world's biggest mountains ends, it will be time to do something different. There are lots of other mountains and other challenges. That's a good thing for me. When you do something because you love to do it, you don't want to stop. Not yet. That's the way I feel.

—ED VIESTURS

8,000-METER PEAKS

1. MOUNT EVEREST: *8,850 meters* | *29,035 feet*
2. K2: *8,611 meters* | *28,250 feet*
3. KANCHENJUNGA: *8,598 meters* | *28,209 feet*
4. LHOTSE: *8,501 meters* | *27,890 feet*
5. MAKALU: *8,481 meters* | *27,824 feet*
6. CHO OYU: *8,201 meters* | *26,905 feet*
7. DHAULAGIRI: *8,167 meters* | *26,795 feet*
8. MANASLU: *8,163 meters* | *26,781 feet*
9. NANGA PARBAT: *8,126 meters* | *26,660 feet*
10. ANNAPURNA: *8,078 meters* | *26,503 feet*
11. GASHERBRUM I: *8,068 meters* | *26,469 feet*
12. BROAD PEAK: *8,047 meters* | *26,401 feet*
13. GASHERBRUM II: *8,035 meters* | *26,361 feet*
14. SHISHAPANGMA: *8,012 meters* | *26,286 feet*

FIRST MOUNTAINEERS TO SUMMIT ALL OF THE FOURTEEN 8,000-METER PEAKS

1. REINHOLD MESSNER *(Italy)* 1986
2. JERZY KUKUCZKA *(Poland)* 1987
3. ERHARD LORETAN *(Switzerland)* 1995
4. CARLOS CARSOLIO *(Mexico)* 1996
5. KRZYSZTOF WIELICKI *(Poland)* 1996

CONVERSION

1 METER: *3.28084 feet* | 1 FOOT: *0.3048 meters*

FIRST ASCENTS

1. MOUNT EVEREST: May 29, 1953 | E. Hillary and T. Norgay
2. K2: July 31, 1954 | A. Compagnoni and L. Lacedelli
3. KANCHENJUNGA: May 25, 1955 | G. Band and J. Brown
4. LHOTSE: May 18, 1956 | F. Luchsinger and E. Reiss
5. MAKALU: May 15, 1955 | J. Couzy and L. Terray
6. CHO OYU: October 19, 1954 | H. Tichy, S. Jöchler, and Pasang Dawa Lama
7. DHAULAGIRI: May 13, 1960 | K. Diemberger, P. Diener, A. Schelbert, E. Forrer, Nima Dorje, Nawang Dorje
8. MANASLU: May 9, 1956 | T. Imanishi and Gyalzen Norbu
9. NANGA PARBAT: July 3, 1953 | H. Buhl
10. ANNAPURNA: June 3, 1950 | M. Herzog and L. Lachenal
11. GASHERBRUM I: July 4, 1958 | P. Schoening and A. Kauffman
12. BROAD PEAK: June 9, 1957 | M. Schmuck, F. Wintersteller, K. Diemberger, and H. Buhl
13. GASHERBRUM II: July 7, 1956 | F. Moravec, S. Larch, and H. Willenpart
14. SHISHAPANGMA: May 2, 1964 | Chinese team led by Hsu Ching

ACKNOWLEDGMENTS

I HAVE MANY PEOPLE TO THANK FOR HELPING ME TO LIVE MY DREAMS. The list is long because I have been fortunate to meet scores of amazing people who will always be a part of what I do. Their support in many different ways strengthens my step and lightens my load. For those I have not mentioned please forgive me as it is not intentional but simply an oversight.

The beginning of this book began as a seed of an idea and I would like to thank those that were the core impetus of its growth: my loving wife, Paula, for her belief in me and her support of my idea; Kevin Mulroy, Editor-in-Chief at National Geographic Books, for enthusiastically encouraging my vision of creating this book; Peter Potterfield, who helped me organize my thoughts and put them on paper; the staff at National Geographic Books whose layout, design, and editing helped create the finished piece; and last but not least Warren Wyatt for his friendship, council, and tireless efforts to make this book all that it could be and more.

This book is filled with images that I have acquired through my 15 year career of climbing in the Himalaya. This career has been possible in large part because of the support and encouragement of many people along the way. I thank them for this and they include the following: My parents, Ingrid and Elmars, who never restricted my ideas of perusing my dreams; my sister Velta for always believing in me; Three great friends in particular that helped me through the lean and early days of my career: Dan Hiatt for teaching me the art of carpentry, giving me employment and support; Dave Magee for his encouragement and letting me live in his basement!; and Steve Swaim for his advice, housing, and employment as a veterinarian; and all the rest of my family and other friends that gave me the physiological support to follow the path of mountaineering as a career.

I thank my teachers and mentors who through lessons, words, and example showed me the way of the mountains and gave me the tools to be a safe and successful climber: Eric Simonson, Phil Ershler, George Dunn, Tracey Roberts, Lou Whittaker, Jim Whittaker Peter Whittaker, Joe Horiskey, Jim Wickwire, John Roskelly, Nawang Gombu, and many of the senior guides at Rainier Mountaineering to mention a few. My climbing partners past and present: Richard King who together with a Goldline Rope, tennis shoes, and trial and error we learned rock craft; Curt Mobley with whom I first experienced the alpine peaks of the Cascades and who provided instruction and transportation-both of which I needed; the incomparable Veikka Gustafsson with whom during the last nine years I have shared many great adventures, laughs, and beers; and a host of others with whom I have shared a rope—Andy Politz, Greg Wilson, Craig VanHoy, Robert Link, Larry Nielson, David Carter, Charles Mace, J.-C. Lafaille, Guy Cotter, Carlos Carsolio, Krzysztof Wielicki, Neal Beidleman, Michael Kennedy, and the late greats with whom I experienced many wonderful moments in the mountains and elsewhere, Rob Hall and Scott Fischer.

There are other friends that have their own unique places in my heart and that require their own special thanks: Gil Friesen—a mentor, friend and source of invaluable advice; David Breashears who believed in my abilities and entrusted me with my role as Deputy Leader of the 1996 Everest expedition and for his continued support and wisdom; Hall Wendel with whom I climbed in many of the world's great ranges and sailed the seas; Geila Hocherman and MZH who supported Scott Fischer and me in our early days as struggling climbers; John and Jody Eastman for their friendship, advice, and assistance as my career unfolded; and last but certainly not least John Cumming, who's vision and insight of having me join the gang at Mountain Hardwear was the turning point in my career, which gave me the strength and confidence to pursue my 8,000-meter quest.

My career as mountaineer could not be possible without the invaluable support from my sponsors. My safety and success relies on the quality of their products and my journeys to the mountains requires their financial assistance. I thank them with all of my heart. First and foremost I thank everyone at Mountain Hardwear for taking me into the fold ten years ago and making me a part of their amazing family, and my other sponsors and supporters, past and present, in no particular order—Rolex, JanSport, Expedia, Outdoor Research, Oakley, National Geographic, MicroSoft, Schiff, Trango, Princeton Tec, Gregory, Leki, Smartwool, Magellan, Julie Hines and the staff at Creative Revolution, Eureka, L.L. Bean, Petzl/Charlet Moser, Sterling Rope, Kelty, Asolo, Wapiti Woolies, Thorlo, Polo Ralph Lauren, MTV, Dermatone, Tea Ranch, Nabisco, Mars, Brunton, Island Fitness, KAVU, Thule, Malden Mills Polartec Challenge, Nature's Way, Comp USA, Gateway, Sun Catcher, Orvis, Pristine and Kokatat.

I would also like to thank friends and acquaintances that through the years have lent invaluable advice and moral support: Brian Keating, Richard Bangs, Rebecca Martin, Ian Cumming, Jack Gilbert, Charles Minor Kittrell, Steve Marolt, Jon Krakauer, Chris Mathias, Roland Puton, and David Roberts.

I would like to dedicate this book in memory of four brothers of the rope that inspired and affected me, had tremendous vision, and lived their lives with maximum joy and fulfillment: Rob Hall, Scott Fischer, Alex Lowe, and Goran Kropp. May we all strive to live life as fully as they did.

—E.V.

I GREATLY APPRECIATE ED VIESTURS'S FORBEARANCE AND PATIENCE DURING the many hours he spent in the company of me and my turning tape recorder. Ed's articulate remarks became the gripping narratives featured on these pages, and the opportunity to hear the stories again, first-hand, was reward in itself for me.

I'd like to thank editor Johnna Rizzo of National Geographic Books, whose wisdom and good judgement resulted in a project of unique power and quality.

Finally, I'd like to acknowledge Scott Fischer, who in 1989 first alerted me to the fact that Ed Viesturs was a climber of exceptional skill and drive, a figure who would have a worldwide impact. Scott's good heart, his irresistible way with his friends, and his love of mountains live on in those of us who knew him.

—P.P.

PHOTO CREDITS

All photos by Ed Viesturs unless noted.

Pages 6-7: Paula Viesturs; *Page 15:* John Yeager/1990 International Peace Climb; *Page 16:* Krzysztof Wielicki; *Page 36:* George Dunn; *Page 55:* Charles Mace; *Pages 70-71:* Rob Hall; *Page 72:* Ang Tshering Sherpa; *Pages 76-77:* Rob Hall; *Page 90:* David Breashears; *Page 122:* Veikka Gustafsson.

For more information on Ed Viesturs and current progress on his climbs go to www.edviesturs.com

ED VIESTURS' SPONSORS

Himalayan Quest
Ed Viesturs with Peter Potterfield

Published by the National Geographic Society
John M. Fahey, Jr., *President and Chief Executive Officer*
Gilbert M. Grosvenor, *Chairman of the Board*
Nina D. Hoffman, *Executive Vice President*

Prepared by the Book Division
Kevin Mulroy, *Vice President and Editor-in-Chief*
Charles Kogod, *Illustrations Director*
Marianne R. Koszorus, *Design Director*

Staff for this Book
Johnna M. Rizzo, *Editor*
Charles Kogod, *Illustrations Editor*
Carol Farrar Norton, *Art Director*
Alexander Feldman, *Researcher*
Carl Mehler, *Director of Maps*
Matt Chwastyk, James Huckenpahler, Joseph F. Ochlak, Nicholas P. Rosenbach, Gregory Ugiansky, *Map Research, Edit, and Production*
R. Gary Colbert, *Production Director*
Lewis Bassford, *Production Project Manager*
Meredith C. Wilcox, *Illustrations Assistant*

Manufacturing and Quality Control
Christopher A. Liedel, *Chief Financial Officer*
Phillip L. Schlosser, *Managing Director*
John T. Dunn, *Technical Director*

Printing by R. R. Donnelley & Sons, Willard, Ohio. Color separations by North American Color, Portage, Michigan. Dust jacket printing Miken Companies, Inc., Cheektowaga, New York.

One of the world's largest nonprofit scientific and educational organizations, the National Geographic Society was founded in 1888 "for the increase and diffusion of geographic knowledge." Fulfilling this mission, the Society educates and inspires millions every day through its magazines, books, television programs, videos, maps and atlases, research grants, the National Geographic Bee, teacher workshops, and innovative classroom materials. The Society is supported through membership dues, charitable gifts, and income from the sale of its educational products. This support is vital to National Geographic's mission to increase global understanding and promote conservation of our planet through exploration, research, and education.

For more information, please call 1-800-NGS LINE (647-5463) or write to the following address:

NATIONAL GEOGRAPHIC SOCIETY
1145 17th Street N.W.
Washington, D.C. 20036-4688 U.S.A.

Visit the Society's Web site at
www.nationalgeographic.com.

Library of Congress Cataloging-in-Publication Data

Viesturs, Ed.
  Himalayan quest : Ed Viesturs on the 8,000-meter giants / Ed Viesturs with Peter Potterfield.
    p. cm.
  ISBN 0-7922-6884-9
  1. Mountaineering--Himalaya Mountains. 2. Mountaineering--Himalaya Mountains--Pictorial works. 3. Himalaya Mountains--Description and travel. 4. Mountaineers--United States. I. Potterfield, Peter. II. Title.

GV199.44.H55 V54 2002
796.52'2'09095496--dc21

2002037982